THE CRAFT
OF
Sermon
Illustration

W. E. SANGSTER

A Pickering Pa

Pickering and Inglis
Marshall Pickering
3 Beggarwood Lane, Basingstoke, Hants RG23 7LP, UK

Copyright © 1954 by Epworth Press
First Published by Epworth Press 1954
This edition issued by Pickering and Inglis Ltd
Part of the Marshall Pickering Holdings Group
A subsidiary of the Zondervan Corporation
by special arrangement with Epworth Press.

Pickering and Inglis edition 1978.

Reprinted: Impression number
87 88 89 90: 10 9 8 7 6 5

ISBN: 0 7208 0405 1

Printed and bound in Great Britain at
The Camelot Press Ltd, Southampton

*If of these two things you can do only one —
either hear the Mass or hear the sermon — you
should let the Mass go, rather than the sermon.
. . . There is less peril for your soul in not hearing Mass, than in not hearing the sermon.*

BERNARDINE OF SIENA (1380–1444)

*I cannot hear a sermon without being struck by
the fact that amid drowsy series of sentences
what a sensation a historical fact, a biographical
name, a sharply objective illustration makes!
Why will not the preacher heed the admonition
of the momentary silence of his congregation
(and often what is shown him) that this particular sentence is all they carry away?*

RALPH WALDO EMERSON (1803–1882)

Introduction

William Edwin Sangster (1900-1960)
The Craft of Sermon Illustration

Great Britain, and America to a lesser extent, has not known a more compelling preacher than William Edwin Sangster. He served several churches in England before coming to his greatest ministry in the Westminster Central Hall in London, 1939-45, where in Methodism he was the scholar-evangelist of the pulpit. War demands, air raids, and living in shelters with people while writing a doctoral thesis and at the same time maintaining a full preaching schedule make him eminently qualified to write on the effective use of illustrations in preaching.

Much about the use of illustrations in sermons can be learned from this book by a successful modern preacher. This pulpit orator maintains that preaching is still God's chief way of announcing His will to the world. Neither literature, broadcasting, counseling, movies, nor plays can displace preaching in the purpose of God. The preacher's valiant efforts to become what he should be must not be labeled as unimportant nor should they be regarded as futile. Preaching according to Sangster, did things — most important things. With such a guide who can fail to be inspired?

This source book reflects Sangster's perception and insight. It is a compilation of illustrations drawn from his own life and experiences. Sangster felt that each preacher should get his own illustrations and then use them judiciously in delivering Christ's message.

RALPH G. TURNBULL

Preface to the American Edition

THE warm welcome this book has received in England encourages me to hope that it may be of service to preachers in America also. I offer it, however, with some diffidence, because I do not regard myself as an expert and able always to find the perfect illustration, but rather as one whose confidence derives less from his achievements than from the certainty that he is on the right road.

Such illustrations as I have felt constrained to give are mainly my own and I need not apologize, seeing that it is part of my argument that a man ought to get his own illustrations and not take them from other preachers. If, therefore, I had made the book largely a collection of other men's illustrations, I should have contradicted my main contention and defeated my chief end. But I have shrunk, nevertheless, from giving footnote references to my own books, though it may interest some readers to know that the quoted illustrations are drawn mainly from my smaller volumes of occasional addresses: *Why Jesus Never Wrote a Book, He Is Able,* and *These Things Abide.*

My old professor, Rev. Dr. Charles Ryder Smith, and my ever-dependable secretary, Mr. P. E. Found, both deserve my deep thanks.

W. E. SANGSTER

The Westminster Central Hall
London, England

Contents

THE CRAFT
OF
Sermon
Illustration

I

The Place and Use of Illustration

" IT PLEASED God by the foolishness of preaching to save them that believe."

The foolishness of preaching!

What preacher but has felt at times the foolishness of preaching? Words . . . words . . . words! In moments of depression how can he help but contrast his lot with that of those who *do* things: the cabinetmaker, for instance, ankle-deep in the fresh-smelling shavings and fondling with a craftsman's pride a piece of finished work; an architect, seeing his dreams turn into solid stone before his eyes; an engineer listening, with rapture on his face, to the purring of his great machine?

But the foolishness of preaching . . .

" I gave it up," said one man who showed promise for a while of being a prince among preachers. " I gave it up because I felt that it had no more effect upon people than the patter of the rain upon the roof."

Nevertheless, the fact stands. Mysterious as we may judge it to be, it pleases God still, *by the foolishness of preaching,* to save them that believe. That is not to deny for a moment the interrelation of preaching with other means by which conviction concerning Christianity is brought to bear on human minds. No one who has had a cure of souls for any length of time is likely to minimize the effect on a child of a devout home, or the influence on people at any age of contact with a saint, nor yet the direct advocacy of the Holy Spirit in a human heart when He

> ". . . pleads the truth and makes reply
> To every argument of sin."

But, again and again, all this is made vivid, disturbing, meaningful, by a challenging word from a preacher and the will is moved to action when some poor stammerer eagerly leans over his pulpit and offers Christ. We might wish that God had fashioned his universe another way. In blasphemous vanity, we might suppose, with Omar Khayyám, that, if the world were in our making, we could " remould it nearer to the Heart's Desire," but that is all vain speculation. We must accept the universe. On this earth a chief means which God uses to win men and women to himself is preaching. Inevitably, therefore, all that concerns preaching is of an importance hard to exaggerate and perilous to ignore.

First, of course, in importance is the actual *substance* of preaching — the message itself, the matter, the character of the proclamation. How to announce it (with one aspect of which this book proposes to deal) is, in its very nature, secondary. *What* the preacher has to say as a message from the Almighty is clearly the thing that matters most.

It is one of the tragic curiosities of preaching that some men commissioned to give this message seem to have no message to give. Appearing before people with a warrant which they claim to have taken from the pierced hand, they speak without conviction and they are heard without effect. When they have said all, they have said nothing. If a working woman asked a member of their dispersing congregations, in her homely way, " What was he going on about? " not even the intelligent could give an answer.

Nor is this poverty concealed by the most valuable natural gifts of oratory. Those shining gifts will only provoke the damning criticism of Carlyle: " If that man had anything to say, he could say it." The absence of a message makes the preacher a charlatan. Some of the old Hebrew prophets announced their word from God as a " burden." It weighed them down. How much it weighed them down we may test in this way. As we thrust our shoulder beneath their " burden " today, it weighs us down. Slipping within the covers of their book, we feel the relevance of their message to our own times, and, as we face both the claims of God and the obduracy of man, we feel crushed by the weight of the sorrow of God.

If a man has lost — or never felt — the greatness of his message, he does not need instruction in the craft of sermon illustration. The only value that sermon illustrations can have is to light up the solemn grandeur of the message; to make it clear and winsome and capable of being grasped by the mind — and if there is no message, the very effort becomes meaningless. Indeed, it might be worse than meaningless. Some facility in this craft might blind a man — and even his hearers for a while — to the poverty of the situation and, by engaging their appetites with sugary trifles, leave them half unaware that they never had a meal.

But if a man has felt the greatness of the gospel of

Jesus Christ, if the Bible speaks to him and speaks as the word of the living God, if the doctrines of the Church constrain his heart and reason, and he knows that men are false guides who deprecate doctrinal preaching, if he is schooled, moreover, in the philosophy of religion (not giving it a pre-eminence to theology but, on the other hand, not shutting out its just claims), and if, above all else, he wants to cry, " O let me commend my Saviour to you," then that man will despise no discipline that will make him succeed in his awesome toil and he will gladly " scorn delights, and live laborious days " to prove himself a workman that needs not to be ashamed.

Nor — to be perfectly plain — does the craft of sermon illustration require any man to scorn delights and live laborious days. It is fun. It is an occupation of leisure. It rests a mind tired of grappling with heavier things. It is a recreation with which to reward yourself at the end of a weary day.

Let a man give the best of his time for study to quarrying in the Book of God; let him be at pains to prove that the doctrines of the Church are well set in the Scriptures; let him lose no time (as some do) whining that " people are not asking the right questions," but in facing resolutely the questions they *do* ask even though they seem as " elementary " as every Religious Brains' Trust reveals (" Is there a God? " " Does man need a religion? " " Why pray?" " Is this life the end? ") — and he will discover this: that he can use the odd moments of his busy day in learning how to put his point in a homely parable; how to have at call the apposite incident; how to reach swiftly for an honest analogy; and how, in short, to cast a flood of bright light by apt illustrations on what would otherwise be blurred and without sharp edges in the mind of his most earnest hearers.

The craft of sermon illustration is always subservient. It is important that that be borne in mind. The thin ranks of the great preachers include outstanding figures who never mastered this art at all. R. W. Dale said, " An illustration is my despair." Dean Church and F. W. Robertson illustrate rarely. But no man can come within hailing distance of these masters if he does not burn with his message and feel at least a little of what Paul felt when he said, " Woe is unto me, if I preach not the gospel! "

Nevertheless — having put the subject in its proper place — let us be clear that even if the place is subordinate, the theme is not trifling. Nothing about true preaching is trifling. That which can clarify the Word of God, and carry conviction to a hesitating mind, that which can banish doubt and remove impediments from frustrated faith, is not to be airily set aside by anyone.

Many years ago I talked with a man in the town of St. Helens. He had known much trouble. His wife had been an invalid for years and life had posed other and harder problems for him. I gathered from our conversation that he had been much helped by meditating on Paul's thorn in the flesh. " It has been of help to me for years," he said.

Then he went on:

" I heard a sermon on the subject long ago. It was a very ordinary sermon. My attention wasn't fully held until the end.

" Before the preacher closed, however, he gave an illustration. He told of a man who lived in a provincial town and whose love of music was nourished by phonograph records, the best of which he played over to himself again and again.

" One day he invited another music lover to spend an evening with him, and during the evening he made a little experiment with his friend. ' I am going to play the same record twice,' he said. ' Listen carefully and tell me which rendering you prefer.'

" As the music died away his friend said quite positively: ' I preferred the second rendering. It was purer, sweeter. What was the difference? '

" ' Just this,' said his host. ' The first time I played it with a needle, and the second time with a thorn.' "

I make no comment now on the appositeness of the illustration, nor yet on the fact that the use of thorns for playing records on phonographs has since become common. I stress only this. The point of the illustration went into that man and stayed. It interpreted the faith to him through much testing and he was bold to believe that there was a ministry at the heart of his own unlifting troubles because God was in them and God had said, " My grace is sufficient for thee."

Never again could I think lightly on the art of illustration. By this means hard-pressed men and women can be constrained to believe.

Yet, to make the value of this study clear beyond all cavil, it would be well to set down plainly, and in order, precisely what illustrations can do to extend the preacher's power.

1. *They can make the message clear*

However earnestly a preacher may labor to explain his point, if, in its very nature, the point is somewhat abstruse, and if, as is probable, his congregation includes some people not given to hard consecutive thinking, it is almost certain that it will not be clear to them unless he illustrates what he means. Let him reach for an analogy, or throw the truth into a picture, or give an instance of the principle he is enunciating, and both relief and recognition will register on his hearers' faces. It is as though they say with a smile, " We've got it now."

2. *They ease a congregation*

The amount of time that the average public assembly can listen to a sustained argument is strictly limited. Unless a man has before him a company of highly trained minds, he can only subject them to flinty thinking for short periods. They must rest mentally for a moment or two before moving on again.

3. *They make the truth impressive*

Truth as truth is not impressive. It is, all the time, being debased into truisms. When it has become familiar, people greet its announcement with a yawn. Their very expression seems to say, " We have heard all that before."

Illustrations can do something to combat that. By their means truisms sound true and seem significant. The obscure abstract turns into the vivid concrete, and what seemed blurred when stated as a general principle stands out in sharp impressiveness when seen in the particular. People are convinced more by what they *see* than by what they *hear*. Illustrations help them to *see*.

4. *They make preaching interesting*

So much preaching is *dull*. Indeed, a tradition of dullness in preaching has developed in some circles and it seems almost to be taken as a mark of sanctity if the sermon is certain to bore.

Why the thrilling announcement of good news should be calculated to bore people is altogether mysterious, but there can be no serious doubt that the wise, restrained, and discriminating use of illustration is one means by which dullness can be banished from the pulpit.

5. *They make sermons remembered*

Sermons, of course, are not preached to be remembered: they are preached to be *translated*. When they have gone into character they can be cheerfully forgotten, but during the period of translation it is not unimportant that they be remembered.

Illustrations help to make them remembered. If the illustration deserves to be called an illustration, if, that is to say, it does not need to have its explanation appended but carries it in its very heart, the recollection of the illustration will mean the recollection of the point.

Most preachers have had amusing reminders that people remember the illustrations when they remember nothing else. If a man repeats an illustration (and *occasionally* the same incident can illustrate two things), he may be roguishly accused by the less keen among his hearers of repeating a sermon. It will abate his righteous indignation to remember how deep was the impression that the illustration had made!

6. *They help to persuade people*

Not all preaching is preaching for a verdict. The aim of the preacher on some occasions is to buttress tottering faith or explain in more detail a doctrine that is already held in outline in the hearers' hearts. The element of persuasion is present in both these instances, but it is present supremely in evangelical preaching which lays siege to a man's rebellious will.

At any level of persuasion, illustration is the preacher's help. A vivid picture that clarifies thought, or a feelingful story that touches the emotion, both (in their different ways) thrust at the resisting will. A man may evade the point of an argument by half refusing to follow it and almost seize with eagerness on any obscurity in the exposition in order to sidestep the thrust which he shrewdly suspects is coming, but a picture placarded before his eyes is not so easily avoided. He *sees* the point. He cannot escape seeing it. His very struggle against the truth grows feeble. The illustration slips under his guard and wins the victory " he knows not how." Whatever branch of preaching it be, skill in the use of illustration means more power in the effort to persuade.

7. *They make repetition possible without weariness*

No small part of the craft of preaching is to keep saying the same thing in the same sermon without its appearing to be the same. That is uttered neither in cynicism nor in naïveté. A common error of young preachers is to have too much " matter " in a sermon and not to respect the limitations of their theme even when they fancy that they have fixed them. " One sermon, one aim," is a wise rule. All the more reason, of course, why the aim should be a high and worthy one, but, if every sermon carried conviction to the congregation on one important aspect of truth, the power of the pulpit would be immeasurably increased. There is more sense than there seems at first glance in the homiletical rule of the rustic preacher who said, " First I tells 'em what

I'm going to tell 'em; then I tells 'em; and then I tells
'em what I've told 'em."

Here, then, is the difficulty. How can one do this
without weariness to the hearers? How can this important truth be approached from various angles or hung
in different lights so that *fresh* impression is made on impression and conviction carried beyond the very desire
to resist?

Illustration is a chief means to this end. Freshness in
the illustrations skillfully disguises deliberate insistence
on the sameness of the theme. A few swift strokes at the
end reveal the unity that has been in the speaker's mind
all the time, and people and preacher pass almost im-
perceptibly from consideration of one facet of the gospel to adoration of Him who is the Way, the Truth, and
the Life.

If we add to this sevenfold use of illustration minor
adventitious aids which they render, our survey will approach completeness. A congregation, restless for any
reason at the beginning of a sermon, can be arrested at
once with an apposite illustration: something, for example, that sharply poses the problem to be examined,
or puts in pictorial form the good news to be proclaimed.
Or a congregation disturbed by someone fainting in the
crowded pews can be recalled to the high argument by
the adroit use of some analogy that recapitulates quite
briefly what has already been said.

The decorative use of illustrations has been occasionally discussed, but I do not think that it can be seriously
defended. Though an argument can be made out for
preaching as an art (in the sense of " applied art "),[1]

[1] Cf. Dykes, *The Christian Minister,* p. 180.

and though Phillips Brooks defends the ornamental use of illustration and cites Ruskin in his support,[2] the case is unconvincing at the last. The word " art " (when used as synonymous with " fine art ") has associations not easily reconciled with preaching, and though " ornamentation " has wide legitimate spheres, they do not include the pulpit. Preaching is too awe-ful and urgent. Whatever type of preaching it be, so long as it be true preaching it concerns the holiest things with which we have to deal, and the preacher is standing all the while between God and man. Whether, on this occasion, he comes as evangelist to wake the dead in half an hour, or as expositor to open the Word of the living God to those already in this way of life, his responsibility is immense. He must be excused from interest in the *merely* artistic. Eternal issues hang on this commerce of earth and heaven. I doubt if any of the Hebrew prophets would be said by the highly aesthetic to have blown on a silver trumpet — but it was still the trumpet call of God.

If there are still those unconvinced of the place and use of illustrations in sermons, I would crave a final word or two.

Be quite sure that your denial of their use is not a defense of your inability to master this craft. It is simply *not* true to say that neither philosophers nor the deepest preachers use them. The varied methods of exposition used by the profounder philosophers are not our concern at the moment, but it is a demonstrably shallow judgment to suggest that *depth* in preaching can be swiftly measured by the presence or absence of illustra-

[2] Phillips Brooks, *Lectures on Preaching*, p. 175. 1903 edition.

tions and that the fewer the illustrations, the deeper the thought.

Light up your profound thoughts by illustration! Cast into these deep caverns of elemental thinking where you delve the bright beams of homely analogy (as Kant was not too superior to do) and everyone will be the gainer by it — yourself not least. When you cannot put a thing clearly to other people, it is often because it is not clear to you.

Encourage yourself in all your efforts to do this needed thing well by holding the highest Example of all before your eyes. Jesus taught this way. " Without a parable spake he not unto them." [3] A humble man might feel this part of his duty too hard for him (as Dale did), but surely, with our Lord's example before his eyes, only a combination of vanity and blasphemy could convince a man that the matter was beneath his notice.

Nor need we languish long under the sense of inferiority with which this chapter began, and envy the men who *do* things.

Preaching is meant to *do* things.

It is the rule at most theological colleges for the students to preach at least once during their course before their fellow students and their professors. It is something of an ordeal and the criticism afterward is often sharp. In one theological college I know well, it was always taken as a bad sign if the student whose turn had come to preach was summoned immediately the service was over to the principal's study and told to bring his manuscript.

One miserable fellow answered the summons, deposited the manuscript on the principal's desk, and sat

[3] Matt. 13:34.

in a rather frigid silence for a while which neither he
nor the principal broke.

Finally he burst out:

" It *will* do, sir, won't it? It will do? "

" *Do what?* " snapped the principal.

Ah! There it is! *Do what?*

Preaching is meant to do something — the most tre-
mendous and important of all things, and, because illustrations can help preaching to do it, no more need be
said to justify this book.

II

The Types of Illustration

WHAT is an illustration? The temptation is well-nigh irresistible to copy the classical instance of tautology ("an archdeacon is a man who exercises archidiaconal functions") and simply say that an illustration in a sermon is that which illustrates it.

The tautology will be forgiven if it puts us on our guard against excessive classification and keeps the whole subject to the test of plain usefulness. Being in no doubt about the supreme importance of the message he has to deliver, the preacher is concerned now simply with this: "How can I make my meaning perfectly clear?"

Length is no test of an illustration. A phrase can illustrate — or it may take a paragraph. Let a man bear in mind that it must be no longer than is necessary to do its work, and that the more time it takes the more sure he must be of its fitness and necessity, and the question of length can be dismissed for good.

Figures of speech are minor illustrations. Analogy, allegory, fable, parable, historical allusion, biographical incident, personal experience, and anecdote are all illustrations. Some types are harder to find than others. Some are harder to use. All have their own modest technique. Some are hedged about with greater difficulties. Some congregations are more helped by one kind of illustration than another. The type of illustration with which a preacher is most at home depends in no small part on the general cast of his own mind. Yet *variety* in the kind of illustration is part of the secret of freshness.

Let us glance at the various types of illustration each in turn.

1. *Figures of Speech*

Even men who admit that they have no skill at all in the art of illustration make not infrequent use of figures of speech. Metaphor and simile appear in their pages. An illustration can be given in a stroke, if the stroke is masterly enough.

A quarter of a century ago I heard Dr. J. H. Jowett (whose range in illustration was very wide) speaking of Paul's toilsome missionary journeys and of all the persecution he endured. He said, " I once saw the track of a bleeding hare across the snow: that was Paul's track across Europe." For twenty-five years, whenever I have thought on Paul's missionary journeys, I have *seen* the track of a bleeding hare across the snow.

When Henry Drummond was speaking of the toilsome life of the Pharisees " under the law " he said, " In those days men were *working their passage* to heaven by keeping the Ten Commandments." [4] He gives a sharp picture of a whole way of life in those three words.

Fresh and vivid figures of speech can be most useful miniature illustrations.

2. *Analogy*

Nature and life often speak to us with two voices: one loud and heard by all; one quiet and whispered in

[4] Drummond, *The Greatest Thing in the World*, p. 11.

the ear. The education of the ear, not to miss this second voice, is one of the secrets of sermon illustration which we have yet to examine. But it is important to notice now that it is nowhere more useful than in the finding of good analogies. To take some established fact of science, or some phenomenon of nature, and turn it to a clear and just analogical use is a gift that seems natural to certain preachers but which can be developed even in those to whom it seems not to be easy at first. The analogy has its special dangers. Much spurious reasoning has gained currency by false analogies but when an analogy is clearly and truly drawn it is unexcelled in the art of illustration. Deep truth becomes suddenly clear by a homely parallel.

Dr. W. L. Watkinson had great skill in analogies. Many of them were drawn from nature and science. From a hundred examples, these might be taken as typical. Speaking of sudden conversions he says:

" Men of the world do not like these sudden conversions, I know; they feel that there ought to have been a succession of stages, reformations, instructions, preparations; but in treating of embryology scientific men tell us of ' condensed evolution,' of stages taking place and succeeding each other in a few months in the individual, although they occupy millions of years perhaps in the race. Now, if anyone objects to these rapid transformations of sinners into saints, I reply, condensed evolution. That poor wretch in the hovel — condensed evolution; Saul of Tarsus — striking case of condensed evolution; penitent thief — crowning instance of condensed evolution. ' So is every one that is born of the Spirit.' " [5]

Preaching on our foolish human resentment of the laws of God he says:

[5] *The Blind Spot,* p. 91.

" And yet how blindly do we mutiny against the great words of light and love! Some time ago the newspaper related that a herd of cattle was being driven through a long, dark, wooden tubular bridge. Here and there in the planks were knotholes, which let in the sun in bars of light. The animals were afraid of these sun bars; they shied at them, were terrified at them, and then, leaping over them, made a painful hurdle race of it, coming out at the other end palpitating and exhausted. We act just as madly. The laws of God are golden rays in a dark path, they are for our guidance and infinite perfecting and consolation; but they irritate us, they enrage us, we count them despotic barriers to liberty and happiness, and too often we put them under our feet. ' So foolish was I, and ignorant: I was as a beast before thee.' " [6]

3. *Allegory*

The distinctions between the allegory, the fable, and the parable have never been firmly and finally drawn. Fowler in *Modern English Usage* holds that allegory and parable are " almost exchangeable terms." Archbishop Trench in *Notes on the Parables* devotes his first chapter to the definition of the parable, but never *makes* a definition. He labors rather to show how the parable differs from the fable and the allegory, and seeks to bring out its essential character by contrasts.

Our classification requires at least a rough distinction, and we shall make the rough distinction here. All three have a moral and spiritual use for the preacher. We shall use the term *allegory* for those imaginative narratives of spiritual purport in which the vices, virtues, and moral qualities of men are personalized (e.g., Mr. Greatheart, Mr. Obstinate) and in which an emblem is suggestively used to convey a meaning other than the literal one. We shall use *fable* for those stories, obviously not founded

[6] *The Blind Spot*, p. 218.

on fact, in which moral truth is imparted by attributing reason and language to trees, birds, beasts, the elements, etc., and we shall include here also legends and those illustrative stories in which supernatural beings (e.g., angels, devils) play a chief part. We shall use *parable* for stories (which may or may not be founded on fact) that enshrine spiritual truth, and reveal the relations of God to his world (though not by the means of personalizing moral qualities as does the allegory). It is not claimed that these distinctions are complete demarcations, or that this is the precise meaning of the terms as commonly used. But, having regard to the fact that the meanings of these words have no sharp edges in general use, some definition is demanded for clarity in discussion, and these definitions will serve.

Bunyan comes to all informed minds the moment that allegory is mentioned. Allegory was much more favored for illustration seventy years ago than now. It was overused for a generation, handled without skill, entrenched too often on the obvious, and grew wearisome. Psalm 80 and John, ch. 15, are Biblical instances of allegory. *The Pilgrim's Progress* is, of course, the greatest instance outside Scripture. The craft of fashioning a simple, allegorical illustration can be learned by any man of imagination with a feeling for words and by much brooding on Bunyan.

4. *Fable*

The classic fables had, and have, great teaching value. If Aesop was less successful sometimes than others, it will not be denied that his general level is high. Some things can be said in fable form superbly well.

Fables share with the allegory (and normally with the

parable) the demerit of not being true — although, even
here, the distinction must be borne in mind between
what is true to life and what is true to facts. If any useful
comparison can be made between these forms of truth,
it must not be assumed too readily that there is no real
truth that does not tie itself slavishly to happenings.

Not even a child is deceived by a fable. The child
easily understands the simple artifice of it all, and finds
no difficulty in animals that speak and in natural forces
(like the wind and the sun) that reason. Only very
young children fail to grasp the invented character of
it. It is left to adults — and, among them, to the un-
imaginative — to be seriously alarmed at the suggestion
that our Lord's parables, for instance, were stories that
he *made* (or adapted) and that the " certain man " who
had two sons was not necessarily a man whom Jesus
could have named at all. The truth our Lord expressed
in parables is infinitely deeper, of more consequence, and
nearer to our need than the citation of a million facts.
The duck-billed platypus is one of the only two egg-
laying mammals in the world.[7] That is a fact: a most
interesting fact. But what — from the point of view of
man's eternal destiny — does it matter? Parabolic truth
on the lips of Jesus means infinitely more than a thousand expressions of undisputed facts.

The mental atmosphere of our times, it is true, is more
kindly to an illustration built on a scientific fact or a
clear historical allusion, but it should be borne in mind,
nonetheless, that allegory, fable, and parable, which
often do not build on things that actually happened, have
standards of the deepest truth by which they may be
measured. If they are true to life they may be as scornful

[7] The other is, of course, the echidna.

of the charge, as great fiction always has been, that they are not being true to facts.

Before turning, then, to the illustrative use of parables, let us look at the illustrations we have classified under fable. Discussing the ramifications of jealousy in the human heart, a preacher was at pains to point out that it often invades families and finds the most fecund soil where one brother succeeds and the other conspicuously fails. He went on:

" The Devil was once crossing the Libyan Desert when he came upon a group of small fiends who were tempting a holy hermit. They tried him with the seductions of the flesh: they sought to sow his mind with doubts and fears: they told him that all his austerities were nothing worth. But it was all of no avail. The holy man was impeccable. Then the Devil stepped forward. Addressing the imps he said: ' Your methods are too crude. Permit me for one moment. This is what I should recommend.' Going up to the hermit, he said: ' Have you heard the news? Your brother has been made Bishop of Alexandria.' The fable says, ' A scowl of malignant jealousy clouded the serene face of the holy man.' "

Or, as another instance of a little story using supernatural beings to help its artifice, consider this for an illustration of *renunciation* — and notice at the same time its Celtic tang:

" There was a woman of the glens who had an only son; a right proper lad; tall and very fine to look upon. His eyes had the blue of June hills in them. When he spoke his voice gave out a music like that of a little waterfall heard in a still dusk. A girl watched him smile, and found there was no more heart left in her. And boys vowed that his equal was not to be met with among the peopled Isles. All this was he to his lady-mother and more, the dawn and the noon and the sunset of her dream. For, alas, it came to that. Since he went to the

wars and fell. But she died too — not her body, but her courage and her pride and her care for living. And there was no
ebb to her grieving. At last in pity God sent her an angel who
offered the three gifts of comfort that are wont to salve such
as she: the gift that is forgetfulness; the gift of refuge in another's heart; the gift that is his promise of an early meeting
in the upper garden. But she only said the angel nay. ' Tell
the High Father,' she cried, ' that I will heal me of my sorrow when he gives me back my son.' So the angel winged back
to the court of light, sore mourning that she, the lady-mother,
could not see that to give up a dearest thing to God is to
keep it, and that blind are they who close the door upon the
offered riches of love." [8]

5. *Parable*

Precisely what our Lord was saying when the men
sent to arrest him gaped on helplessly in the crowd we
do not know, but we *do* know that they returned un-
successful, bewildered, and most deeply impressed, and
said to their baffled superiors, " Never man spake like
this man." [9]

Whenever we read his parables this word forms itself
in our amazed minds again: " Never man spake like this
man." No one need look for any other Exemplar in this
branch of the art of illustration. The perfect is in full
view.

All the reasons that influenced Jesus in his decision to
teach by parables need not concern us now. That there
is a spiritual strategy about them is clear from the out-
set. Men are on guard against denunciation but nobody
ever guarded himself against a clean storyteller. The
seemingly innocent tale glides into the mind unhindered
and on the lips of a master it needs no explanation. To

[8] Alistair Maclean, *Hebridean Altars*, p. 79.
[9] John 7:46.

moralize is quite unnecessary. The tale ends and conscience stabs *from within*.

If we leave aside the disputed instance of the Sower [10] (and never did the disciples seem more dense), and also the parable of the Wheat and the Tares,[11] Jesus never had need to explain his parables. A well-made parable well told needs no explanation. Indeed, it may be taken as one of the tests: " Does it explain itself? " If one or two of the parables seem hard for us to understand now, it may be doubted whether the people of spiritual discernment among those who first heard them really found them so.

Nor will the thoughtful student of our Lord's parables miss their *homeliness;* not one of them is farfetched.[12] Nor will he miss the amazing economy in words that Jesus exercised. It is impossible to shorten the parables without impairing the sense. Every word — every *little word* — carries its own freight of added and pithy meaning. Consider, for example, in the parable of the Prodigal Son the force of the words " far," " great," " ran," " best " [13] and — in the same parable — the subtlety and point of such contrasted words as " kid " and " calf " and " thy son " and " thy brother."

The peerlessness of these parabolic examples will prove something of a deterrent to the normal student. He will say — and say truly — " It is high, I cannot attain unto it." But then he will go on . . . and find this: that for some homiletic purposes no illustration can surpass the parable and — piecing together this and that, using bits

[10] Matt. 13:3–23.
[11] Matt. 13:36 ff.
[12] Some scholars would regard the parable of the Rich Man and Lazarus as an exception to this rule.
[13] Luke 15:11–32.

of experience and bits of imagination — he will grow in power to make his own parables and to portray truth in this divinely employed manner, finding an entrance for it at lowly doors.

6. *Historical Allusion*

Theists believe that there is an *inwardness* to history. Events — world events — can be regarded either from the manward or the Godward side. They can be considered as the results entirely of human wills (their conflicts and harmonies, their strivings and obstructions) but also as an unfolding of the plan of God — sometimes *with* men and sometimes *against* them — but always for man's highest good.

The power to read history as the Hebrew prophets read it is rare and by no means to be confused with numerology, astrology, pyramidology, and other quasi cults. It is emphatically not a sphere for the dabbler. The man who thinks it easy might well pause to consider that H. A. L. Fisher, after a lifetime of historical study, failed to find any unfolding purpose in it at all.[14]

But the preacher of the Christian gospel deeply believes that it is there. He believes that he can show " the fulness of the time " in which God sent forth his Son born of a woman. The link between the Renaissance, the Reformation, and the invention of printing is plain to him. He sees no accident in the action and reaction and interaction of the Evangelical Revival and the Industrial Revolution. God is in this world, working through it, expressing himself in events, passing judgment on its doings, and giving guidance in one generation for all the discerning in the next. The power to make masterly

[14] *A History of Europe,* Preface, p. v.

comparison, to draw illuminating inferences, to read God's righteous sentence on a whole age, requires a range of knowledge and a depth of insight possessed by few.

Yet even the man of modest equipment is not shut out. When the fruits of national sin begin to appear they are blatant. They cry aloud to heaven. Men without encyclopedic knowledge can scan the page of past history and draw the illustration which they need. They will beware of being always in a denunciatory mood and constantly scolding a congregation for sins other than the sins it commits. But, important as it is in most sermons to give an individual application of the point one is making, there is a duty attaching to the pulpit to interpret God's will to the age, to take broad sweeps, to make wide but pertinent comparisons, and to see things nationally and internationally as well. Historical illustrations are demanded by this duty in preaching, and he is a happy man who can move with confidence in these realms and marshal the facts he needs. F. W. Robertson, in his Advent sermons of 1849, can be seen surveying history from the viewpoint of the Christian preacher — Greek, Roman, and Barbarian [15] — and, a year later, turning the same scrutinizing glance over the history of Israel as well.[16]

7. *Biographical Incident*

Nothing interprets life like life. The art of living is well studied by examining the way that men and women have lived.

The preacher affirms that such and such a line of conduct is almost bound to issue in certain results. For

[15] *Sermons: First Series*, pp. 162–204.
[16] *Sermons: Fourth Series*, pp. 287–296.

example, to marry half convinced that you are not suited to the person you mean to make your partner is to disregard your own judgment and almost certain to issue in unhappiness. The congregation is only mildly interested and may even be contesting the assertion in their minds. He goes on:

"Think of Edward FitzGerald, the translator of *The Rubáiyát of Omar Khayyám*, who married not for affection but to befriend a deceased friend's daughter because he believed that a woman of pride would be willing to accept from a husband what she would not be willing to accept from a friend. Think of Abraham Lincoln who, having once already withdrawn from marrying Mary Todd, halfheartedly 'goes through with it' at the last, and writes to a friend five days after the wedding, 'Nothing new here, except my marrying, which, to me, is a matter of profound wonder.' Think of Charles Dickens and his long remonstrances to his sweetheart about her moods and humors and his solemn warning that 'that which you make no effort to conceal from a lover will appear more frequently before the eyes of a husband.' All these marriages broke down."

What part this would have in the argument of the sermon as a whole we need not pause now to inquire, but it puts the preacher's point. He states his thesis and, because it is not enough just to state a conviction which others will contest, he underlines it with three swift strokes. The argument has still to proceed but the point for which he is contending is plain for all to see.

Or, suppose that the preacher is raising the question as to what effect upon a man's work for God the defects in his own character may have; what better way can he focus the question for people than to pile up rapidly instances of what he means? For example: " the hot temper of Bishop Selwyn," " the egoism of Joseph Parker," " the autocracy of William Booth."

A wide, intimate, and exact knowledge of biography is indispensable for this type of illustration. Not that everything written about a man will necessarily be accepted as true. The student will know how to pick his way between the biography of the sycophant and the biography of the traducer, and a man claiming to utter the truth of God will be at pains to get as near to the truth concerning the men he mentions as he possibly can.

How to range over these wide fields, and store this honey, is a question to which we have yet to turn but it will be enough at the moment to recognize what the honey is that we want.

Nor is the use of the biographical material confined to the swift stroke we have employed above. Every aspect of life is covered by life. Every situation a preacher might want to discuss has its counterpart somewhere in biography.

A minister was speaking one day about the pathos of growing old. He had in mind the transience of life's palmy days. He needed an illustration — and he knew just where to put his hand on what he wanted. It was in Edward Bok's autobiography. He said:

" Edward Bok, the well-known American editor, tells a similar story. When he was a lad he visited Emerson in order to beg a signature for his autograph album from that distinguished man. On being ushered into the presence of the great man, Emerson looked at him with a vacant eye and seemed incapable of understanding why the boy had come. ' Name? ' he said vaguely. ' You want a name? ' ' Write out the name you want,' he said finally, ' and I will copy it for you if I can.' Greatly bewildered, Bok sat down and wrote ' Ralph Waldo

Emerson,' and letter by letter, with constant reference to the original, the old man copied his own name in the boy's book. Earth's palmy day was far behind.

> " ' The will has forgotten the life-long aim,
> And the mind can only disgrace its fame,
> And a man is uncertain of his own name.' "

The theme was " forgiveness " on another occasion. Merely to extol the virtues is not enough. They glow in the hearers' hearts when they are fittingly illustrated. Wide reading in biography puts them all at hand.

" But perhaps no instance of sublime forgiveness comes quite so near the spirit of Calvary as that of Edmund Campion, the English Jesuit. Finest of all the followers of Loyola who suffered for their faith in England, he has been praised by Protestants and Roman Catholics alike. In the days when his coreligionists were persecuted in this country, he perilously moved from place to place, nourishing their spiritual life, and narrowly avoiding arrest. But he was caught at last. Betrayed by one of his own people turned apostate, he was thrown into the Tower of London and thrice tortured on the rack. But nothing could shake either his constancy or serenity, and he heard his sentence to be hanged, drawn and quartered at Tyburn, with the calmness of a man whose whole life was stayed on God. He actually broke into the Te Deum.

" A day or two before his execution, he had an amazing visitor. The spy who had betrayed him, and who knew his own life to be in hourly peril from the rage of old friends who had learned of his part in the arrest, staggered into Campion's cell, behind a jailer, and begged to be forgiven. The condemned man was weak from torture, and anticipating Tyburn, but he did not hesitate. He fully and freely forgave him. Still the traitor lingered. Would the gracious father do more? Would he help him escape from the fury of his pursuers? Even this the betrayed man was ready to do. Without a word of rebuke, he promised him a letter of introduction to a German nobleman who would accept his service, and on a rainy December morning he was tied to a hurdle and dragged from the Tower to Tyburn, through the filth and garbage of the London gutters. No hate, no bitterness, no lust for revenge. He went up the cart at the place of execution as though he were going to a wedding. In that last dread hour, poise and equanimity marked all that he did, and they were the fine fruit of his faith, his clear conscience, and his magnanimous forgiveness."

8. *Personal Experience*

No illustrations need to be used with more restraint than personal experiences. I do not mean personal *observations* — which is a wide source of illustration, as we shall stress in the next chapter — but personal *experiences* where, in the nature of the case, the stress falls on oneself, one's thoughts, one's doings.

Talking overmuch about oneself is a fearful fault in a preacher and it is hardly less heinous when he constantly talks about his own wife and children. The path, alas! is made slippery for him by the undoubted worth of personal testimony to the grace of God, but when a man yields so completely to this that he is always talking, for example, of his own conversion (and seeming to imply that that is the *one* way into the Kingdom), or constantly lecturing on his own life story (as is the way of certain itinerant evangelists), something serious has happened to that man. We are not really so important as that. Clearly such people have forgotten the wise rule: " Seven words about Him for every word about myself."

Nevertheless, there is a moment for giving a personal experience and — wisely used — it can be a very great moment. Let a man be doubly careful to scrutinize any illustration in which he figures prominently himself, let him question his own heart whether or not this be an occasion where nothing would be lost if the experience could be given as " someone's " experience, and disguised in its autobiographical character, let him be sure that this *is* a time when God wills that he disclose some chamber of his own private life and, being sure, let him speak — and there will be a power about it which few will miss. The very rarity of his self-disclosures will add power to the instances when they occur. His known disinclination to display his own soul in public will leave his hearers in no doubt as to his opinion of the importance of the simple illustration and it will be heard with the respect that it deserves.

No one, so far as I am aware, ever seriously accused Dale of Birmingham of parading himself. When Joseph Chamberlain was taunted in the House of Commons with being " the member for Dr. Dale " he swiftly retorted that he wished every member represented so fine a constituency. One of Dale's rare illustrations might serve as an example of the power of a personal experience fittingly told. Dale was speaking of the encouragement which often lies in a little word. He had been ill himself and was feeling, perhaps, in his weakness, a passing weariness in well-doing. This doughty champion of social righteousness was not above the benison of a grateful word. He said:

" There are times when the most buoyant sink into despondency, when a gray, chilly mist creeps over the soul of those who have the largest happiness in the service of God, and then they feel as if all their strength was gone. Not very long ago — if I may venture once more to speak of myself — one of these evil moods was upon me; but as I was passing along one of the streets of Birmingham, a poor but decently dressed woman, laden with parcels, stopped me and said, ' God bless you, Dr. Dale! ' Her face was unknown to me. I said, ' Thank you, but what is your name? ' ' Never mind my name,' she answered; ' but if you could only know how you have made me feel hundreds of times, and what a happy home you have given me! God bless you! ' The mist broke, the sunlight came, I breathed the free air of the mountains of God." [17]

" Testimony " was a preacher's theme when he made use of the following personal illustration. He was stressing the point that we are not always aware how far our witness may reach, and words that seem lost on the air often have astonishing usefulness. He said:

" I was preaching in Plymouth some time ago. I lived in Leeds at the time. Wandering a little disconsolately around a city in which I have few friends, I decided to slip into a telephone call-box and have three minutes' conversation with my wife. It is a long way from Plymouth to Leeds and as I waited for the operator to thread the call through the various exchanges of the Midlands — supposing the line to be sealed — I murmured verses of favorite hymns to myself to while the time away.

> " ' My knowledge of that life is small,
> The eye of faith is dim;
> But 'tis enough that Christ knows all,
> And I shall be with Him.'

Suddenly — from somewhere in the Midlands — a voice vibrant with unspeakable sadness startled me broad awake by calling out over the line: ' Say it again. Say it again.'

" I held the instrument more firmly and said with immense earnestness:

> " ' My knowledge of that life . . .'

As I finished the verse, the same piteous voice called back: ' Thank you! Thank you! '

" Cast on the air . . . and picked up! Uttered in all un-

---

[17] *Fellowship with Christ,* pp. 301 f.

consciousness that it could be overheard, and it became a blessing. It is a picture of how God employs our witness. He contrives his own use of what we do. Many an obscure disciple has lived a life of winsome loveliness all unaware that he was watched, heard, appreciated. . . ."

9. *Anecdote*

Some sermon stylists would banish the anecdote entirely from the pulpit. Nothing, they feel, can prevent it from being " cheap."

They are too severe. The anecdote has its place. It may be distinguished from the biographical incident for the purposes of our rough classification in that the truth of the story is not verifiable in any dependable biography, and either does not attach itself to a great name at all or does so very dubiously. The little story is told with less interest normally in the person to whom it happened than in what it was that occurred. If there is something characteristic in the reaction and, therefore, revealing of the type that figures in the story, if the incident, trifling in itself, serves nonetheless to lift up a mirror to life, it has its value for the preacher and is a mode of illustration he cannot afford to scorn.

The dangers of this type of illustration are legion. Anecdotes are often long, and demanding, therefore, in the time they take to tell. They often incline to sentimentality (as distinguished from sentiment) and increase in repulsiveness to people of taste the more sentimental they become. Often they are a little " odd " in character and express reactions in people that are *not* typical, leaving the hearers feeling that while this may have been said on one occasion, or that done on some other, it is not how *they* would have acted. . . . At its worst, it entrenches on the bizarre.

How to handle the anecdote will be an object of our further study but, in face of all its faults, it must have a place in any classification of sermon illustrations that aims to be comprehensive. If a man tries to get the truth of the things that he relates, if he knows that he cannot exaggerate to the glory of God (!), if he brings high standards to any story that claims admission to his sermon and measures its value against the time that it will take to tell, he will not join the ranks of those pseudo preachers who enter their anecdotage whenever they enter the pulpit, and who have prostituted the solemn task of preaching to a series of sentimental, inane, and dubiously connected tales.

A preacher was raising the problem of " values " when he opened his sermon with the following anecdote:

" It was just after ten o'clock on the night of April 14, 1912, that the *Titanic*, the largest vessel then afloat, crashed in mid-Atlantic into an iceberg, and four hours later went to the bottom. Much has been written of all that took place in those four hours. Survivors spoke of the calm heroism of the captain, the officers, and the crew. They told also of the courage of the bandmaster who played ' Nearer, My God, to Thee,' while he struggled into his life belt, and they said that many women, who could have been rescued, refused the offer, preferring to drown with their husbands.

" They told another story also, less courageous but more curious than any of these.

" A certain woman, who had been allotted a place in one of the boats, asked if she might run back to her stateroom, and she was given three minutes to go. She hurried along the corridors already tilting at a dangerous angle, and crossed the saloon. Money and costly gems littered the floor. Some who snatched at their jewelry spilt it as they ran. In her own stateroom she saw her treasures waiting to be picked up. She saw — and took no heed. Snatching at three oranges which she knew to be there, she took her place in the boat.

" That little incident is instructive. An hour before, it would have seemed incredible to that woman that she could have preferred a crate of oranges to one small diamond, but Death boarded the *Titanic* and, with one blast of his awful breath, all values were transformed. Precious things became worthless: worthless things became precious. Oranges were more than diamonds."

An anecdote of the war provided a preacher with the picture he wanted in order to show that we see ourselves only when we see ourselves in Christ.

" During the war a soldier picked up on the battlefields of France a battered frame which had once contained a picture of Jesus. The picture had gone but the frame still bore the words *Ecce Homo*. The soldier sent it home as a souvenir, and someone at home put a mirror in it, and hung it on the wall. One day a man went into that house and understood the startling words, *Behold the man,* and saw *himself*. We see ourselves only when we see ourselves in Jesus. Blots we barely knew were there come to view in his white light."

No illustrations look their best out of their setting — any more than precious stones do. That is why some artists have a rule never to show a canvas to a prospective buyer except in a frame. But the practiced eye knows how to allow for the mount both in a jewel and a picture, and — we may add — in a sermon illustration too.

III

The Sources of Illustration

TUCKED away on the bookshelves of many preachers —
both ordained and lay — there is an encyclopedia of
moral and religious illustrations. The man may have
bought it himself, or received it as a gift from an ad-
miring member of his congregation. He may make much
use of it — or little. What advice should we give concerning this " treasury " of anecdote and improving
tales?

We should advise that he burn it — or send the paper
to be repulped and put to better use.

No doubt some of these volumes are slightly better
than others. No doubt, also, a man earning his bread all
the week at some other vocation, and winning time for
sermon preparation only with difficulty, has found occasional help in their pages. No doubt, too, the man who
has come to rely upon this kind of crutch will make a
spirited defense of his particular volume, and cite instances of the " gems " he has picked up in this way. If
he is old, or his mind has atrophied, he may need the
crutch till he dies.

When I was at the beginning of my ministry, a kindly
vicar in the neighborhood in which I worked (genu-
inely anxious to help a young man) took me into his

study and shared with me the secret of swift sermon preparation.

" You need only two books," he said. " Here are mine."

One was a volume entitled (I think) *Five Hundred Sermon Ouilines;* the other, *Six Thousand Moral and Religious Anecdotes.*

" Now you work by the indexes," he said. " Just select the outline you want: they are arranged conveniently for the Church year. Then, having fixed your theme, turn up the key word in the *Encyclopædia of Illustrations,* and fit the stories in as required. An hour should see the sermon done."

I have never been able to feel scorn for the vicar as a man because his intentions were so kindly, but more pitiable advice to a young preacher it would be hard to imagine. No defense can be made for these encyclopedias of illustrations or volumes of sermon outlines. Commending the former was one of the least useful pieces of advice that Spurgeon gave to his students.[18] Any man called to be a preacher, and determined to be a serious craftsman in his holy calling, can have no truck with books like these.

Illustrations often have a queer way of " dating " — and most of the matter in the encyclopedias is already out of date. In any case, they are not your own: found, shaped, chiseled, saved by you. The more attractive of the illustrations in published collections are certain to get hackneyed. A man who uses them can never be sure, therefore (especially in churches where the preachers change frequently), that the same illustration has not

[18] Spurgeon, *Lectures to My Students (Third Series)*, pp. 71–143, 178–189.

been used the week before. Arthur Porritt tells of the amusing repetition of a certain children's address by visiting preachers at the church that he attended:

" Some time ago, when the church I attend was without a minister for about a year, we had a procession of ' supply ' preachers through the pulpit. One after another told, as a children's address, a story about a little boy who presented his mother with a bill for 2s. 6d. setting out the charges for running errands, chopping wood, cleaning knives, and other odd chores. The mother paid the 2s. 6d., but along with the cash presented her bill — ' for caring for Fred for nine years, feeding him, clothing him, nursing him, taking him on holidays, etc., £o os od.' It was quite a nice little moral story, and on first hearing was very effective. But as one ' supply ' preacher after another told the story its luster dimmed, and at last we found it interesting to watch for variations in the items in the boy's bill. Eventually, when a good friend of my own, Rev. J. G——, supplied the pulpit, and began his children's address with the threadbare tale, there were smiles all over the church. Next day I met J. G., in a restaurant, and congratulated him on his children's address. He seemed pleased. Then I added: ' Well, I'll put it this way — of all the ten men who have told that story from our pulpit in the last twelve months, you told it the best.' " [19]

Let a man determine to get his own illustrations. Let him master the way of it as early in his preaching career as possible. Let him gather constantly — and *enjoy* the gathering — and the morning will come when he will wake up with surprise and realize that his diligence with odd moments has laid up a store of things so good, and so varied, that there is no theme on which he is likely to preach — and no aspect of a theme — for which he

[19] *The Best I Remember,* pp. 234 f.

could not find quite readily the best illustrative material:
fresh, apt, exact, and throwing a flood of light on the
subject he has in mind.

Educating one's intuition for the sound illustration is
a primary task. Every preacher has some sense of what
is fitting to light up the road he wants his hearers to
travel. This sense must be sensitized, disciplined, kept
alert. Life will do the rest. Illustrations crowd upon us
every day. The alert, sensitive, disciplined mind just
takes them in.

Some experiences of life, or incidents met with in
one's reading, almost announce themselves as illustrations right away. They announce also what it is that they
illustrate. " What a perfect example of forgiveness," you
think, and you note it at once, and note it for that use,
However good your natural memory, you note it in pen
and ink. It is true that the habit becomes slavish but it
is not greedy of time. The note is soon made. The vanity
of supposing that you could *never* forget a thing so good
must be cured — and cured early. You *can*. You have
already lost a thousand treasures that way. You cannot
afford to lose more.

But some of the best things you will meet will not
announce themselves in that obvious way. They will
speak in what I have called two voices: one loud and
heard by all; one whispered in the ear. This is especially
true of analogies — a most valuable type of illustration.
You will note the thing in itself, and then you will note
that it seems to be saying something else as well. What
the " something else " is you cannot make out at the
moment. But you are certain it is there.

Respect that intuition! Note the thing! Put it down — not for itself chiefly, but for the other inarticulated truth it is seeking to say.

Later — at your leisure — take it out and look at it. Sit patiently in front of that observed fact, or remembered phrase, and question it: " What are you saying to me? "

Don't think about any particular sermon at this time. That is well-nigh fatal. It will " pull " the illustration off its course. Question it as though you are never going to preach another sermon in your life, and, in the manner of a serious scientist questioning nature, inquire what the analogical lesson is. If it is stubborn, be patient. Put it away — and then, later, catch it unawares. It will not resist you forever. At the last, it may come in a flash. " This is what I illustrate," it will say, and the moment you see it all doubt will go. The glow of conviction will be in you. It was born to say that.

Reserve the illustration for that use. However hard pressed you may be, hold it for that purpose. Let it wait five years if necessary until that theme — and that aspect of that theme — lays hold on you. Be sure that its hour will come.

Any man who has heard a master of sermon illustration state his point, argue it, perplex the congregation perhaps by its difficulty, and then gloriously extricate them by a perfect illustration, any man who has seen the members of a congregation almost smile their simultaneous gratitude when the point has gone right home — how can he help wondering where that illustration came from: so exact, so finished, so " inevitable "?

It was just like that with Dr. W. L. Watkinson.

Many a prentice preacher, listening to that master of the art, must have asked himself: " How did he do it? How did he think of anything so perfect for his purpose between Friday night and Sunday morning? "

The short answer, of course, is that he didn't. Perfect illustrations are not thought of between Friday night and Sunday morning, or even Tuesday night and Sunday morning. The preacher had them; stored them; saved them for their inevitable hour. The hour came. He polished his jewel, shaped the mount, and put it in.

Now and then a glorious illustration *will* come to a man late, within an hour or two of preaching; occasionally, even on his feet. But this is rare — and even then the flashes come to those who are sensitive to the value of illustrations, alert for them, and definitely not relying on sudden inspiration. Beecher, who lifted some of his illustrations off the faces of the members of his congregation while he was in the very act of preaching,[20] prepared the larger number of them beforehand. In any case, Beecher was no normal man's guide in preaching. He " prepared " each sermon *just* before delivering it — and both, therefore, on Sunday.[21] Many of his illustrations he repeated over, and over, and over again. Genius seldom has " methods," and even then they are not to be copied. Nor did Beecher's genius lie specifically in the art of illustration.

Here is the plain path for the normal man. Let him educate his own modest intuition for the sound illustration. Let him rejoice to find it grow in power and perception. Let him recognize that if he is hard pressed for an illustration, and needs to scrabble round for it at the

[20] *Lectures on Preaching*, pp. 189 f. 1872 edition.
[21] *Ibid.*, pp. 226 f.

last moment, he is almost certain to press something not highly suitable into his importunate use. Let him resolve that when he cannot illustrate his point well, he will not illustrate at all.

Nor need he fear to meet all the demands that will be made upon him and to meet them with more ease with passing time. Many a young minister, facing the same congregation twice a Sunday, and for nearly fifty Sundays in the year, has wondered where all the material was coming from to meet this demand, and meet it well. If, to the actual matter of his sermons, he now adds a concern about the illustrations that will be necessary to light the matter up, a new worry may be born in him. Where are all these apt and fresh illustrations to come from? How can he hope to be equal to this constant demand?

He need not worry. If he educates his intuition for illustration, he need *never* look for them. They will look for *him*. They will seek him out, and " give themselves up." Every normal day, and many times a day, they will swim in upon him. He has nothing to do but to put the net down and haul them in. An educated intuition, and a firm rule to pick up *at once* whatever is offered, is all he needs. Having these, he has no ground for fear. No time need be stolen from his serious study: not one hour less with the Bible, or theology, or the philosophy of religion; not one hour less for visitation, or the personal spiritual guidance of his people by individual interview in his vestry. Illustration will be just a pleasant by-product, and a way of rewarding himself when heavier work is done. He will enjoy it for itself alone but, most of all, for its incomparable aid in making the message clear and plain.

On this view, therefore, there are no *sources* of illustration in the sense that one must make regular journeys to certain places of specific purpose to get certain things. Not at all! But there are certain times, and certain mental occupations, and certain fields, in which one should be especially alert, and it would be well if we looked at those fertile fields now.

1. *The Bible*

The Bible is in a category all its own, not only as a book, but as a source of sermon illustrations. It is not read as once it was. Despite the pleasing popularity of Bible-reading fellowships, we should be mistaken to suppose that the Book is known to this generation as it was known to the previous one.

The preacher can turn that loss into gain. A generation ago, a minister illustrating from the Bible could be fairly sure that a considerable number of his hearers were familiar with his illustration before he could get it said. By the nature of the case, it lacked freshness, and might even be hackneyed.

He is not in that embarrassment today. The Bible, alas! to many people (even in the churches) is not a familiar book. All the more need, therefore, that he should use it freely for lighting up his theme.

And what a mine it is! Almost every kind of illustration that we have distinguished is to be found here. What use of history! What a wealth of biographical material vivid, penetrating, revealing! What stories — the trial of Abraham, Joseph and his brethren, Samson, Ruth and Naomi, the call of Samuel, the anointing of David, Goliath of Gath, the death of Absalom, Naaman and Gehazi. Nor is it only narrative: parable, allegory, and analogy, all are here. Nothing lights up the New Testament like the Old. If a man picked up just one volume of Alexander Whyte's *Bible Characters* to learn what could be done to interpret life today by life in Biblical times, he would be amazed at the treasure already at his hand.

To whet people's appetite for the Bible is a great aim in itself. To send them home eager to read themselves a Book that so clearly yields such rich things to their minister is a notable success. Anything that a preacher of the gospel would take as illustrative material from the Bible will have an added value which no other volume can possibly possess. If, for any reason that seemed good to him (though there is no need for such self-denial), a man were to limit his illustrations to only one field, it must be this. In the sense in which Wesley meant it (though only in that sense) we might all vow to be *homo unius libri*.[22] This first of books — this book which occupies a category by itself alone — is first in all fields of illustration both in the awesomeness and authority which belong at all times to the Word of God, and also in the fecundity of the yield.

If, in this study, we give more space to other sources of illustration, that must not be interpreted as challenging the pre-eminence which must ever belong to the Book of Books.

2. *Observation*

All nature and all life, we have said, are rich in illustration. As one sails through life with a trawling eye, what fine things come into the net!

I go for a walk and notice that the clock in the rustic

[22] *Works* (1771), par. 4 of the General Preface.

church tower has only one hand. It always had one hand. It belongs to the days when all clocks had one hand. It is the small hand, of course. One must guess at the minutes.

" It looks like half past three, but it might be twenty past, and it might be twenty to four. That is the nearest the old clock can do.

" There is a note in the church about the clock. It has been telling the time, it seems, in the village for five hundred years. Telling the time! — well . . . as near as it can! And it has been near enough in this rustic place.

" What else has it been telling besides the time? There's something else in this. . . .

" Ah! I have it. ' Do the best with what you've got.' Not a bad thing to say to fifteen generations. ' Do the best with what you've got.' The old clock didn't give up when two-handed clocks came in. It went on doing the best it could with one poor hand. What perseverance in limited service! Is there a link here with the parable of the Talents? Maybe! I'll think it out tonight. . . .

" And, while I'm here, I might as well glance at the sundial. I've found a few useful things on sundials.

" What is this? *Traveler, it is later than you think.* Solemn word! Perhaps it is. I keep kidding myself that I'm only a boy and that the sun is still climbing the sky, but there is gray hair in the comb now. . . . ' Later than I think.'

" I must sound that note sometime in an end-of-the-year sermon. I'll tell them what the sundial says. ' Later than you think.'

" I must go. This church is a nice old place. I must come back sometime. But what is this on a tombstone

by the gate? It is to somebody's mother. How well put!
' The mother of many children, one of whom alone had
the misfortune to survive her.' Isn't that what Thomas
Gray said about *his* mother? But who could blame this
rustic son for stealing anything so sweet?

" I shall be talking on mothers sometime. Mothering
Sunday, perhaps. Mid-Lent! It is not in the Church cal-
endar, any more than harvest festivals, but not to be
despised because of that. It will do no man any harm
to be reminded of his good mother."

It has been a rule of my life for years, whenever I am
visiting a neighborhood new to me, to look up before
going the historical and literary associations of the dis-
trict, and to inquire how the people earn their bread.
When I arrive, I know what I want to see. Indeed, when
necessary, I have sought permission beforehand, and I
look back through the years over a thousand enjoyable
and instructive hours spent in that fashion. But it is for
enjoyment that I squeezed the time. I am curious, and
like spending my hard-won leisure that way. Before the
duties of the day begin; between two engagements, or
when work is over . . . what journeys through the past,
what recollections of literary masterpieces, and what
deepened understanding of how folk live! I do not go
on these errands looking for illustrations. I *never* look
for them. But it is in those hours (among others) that
they come offering themselves to me. Shoals of them!
Like a rueful angler, I point with some pride to my
catch, but I am also smartingly aware of the big ones
that got away.

Carisbrooke Castle in the Isle of Wight! Lost in a
reverie in the little museum there, and with my mind

threading the long avenues of the historic past, thinking
of sieges and sorties, of Henry I, Elizabeth, and Charles I,
I remember being brought to earth by a charwoman on
holiday who panted in (bless her!) with her shoes over-
full of feet, and, taking one look at the suits of armor
which had thrilled me, she said to her friend: " Oh,
look at that! Fancy having to clean that every week!! "

The same object presented to two different minds, yet
opening at once on two different worlds. I looked at her
gnarled, knobbly hands, toilworn, and clearly fight-
ing a losing battle with rheumatism, and I loved her as
one of the workers of the world.

And it was at Carisbrooke also that I saw a donkey
drawing water from the well — just turning in circles;
getting nowhere; only going round and round.

I have known saints of God like that. " Silly don-
keys " to the smart. Getting nowhere! Doing nothing.

But in the parched periods that have fallen on my
own soul, I have known that it was to them and not to
the wisecrackers that I must turn if I was to get a cold,
refreshing drink on a hot and arid day.

Tattershall, Bodiam, Bamburgh, Conway — these and
a hundred others all paid their tribute, though, even
then, not so richly as the abbeys and the priories have
brought it in. Christchurch (and its fascinating chancel
arch); Boxgrove (and its *empty* chantry), Rievaulx,
Bylands, Fountains, Tintern, all gave me something —
already used, or resolutely kept till its appointed hour.

Old buildings mean very little to some men. It bores
them to read the record of the past, and architecture
makes no moving appeal.

It does not matter — or not much! Every man to his
taste. The person who thinks that my interest in a bit

of old wall is odd may be deeply interested, and quite surprisingly informed, on marine zoology. A walk on the beach will give him a score of illustrations all hidden, alas! to me.

Let a man follow his own bent. He will illustrate best from the things he knows best. He must be on his guard, of course, against overriding his hobby horse, and talking too often of the things that chance to please him. The subordinate place of illustration must never be forgotten. One has known preachers with a special taste for science, or fine art, or geology, or Wordsworth's poems, who seemed incapable of preaching without dragging (the word is deliberate) their special interest in. However unaware of it the good man may be himself, it becomes a joke among the people who constantly hear him preach.

Variety in the *types* of illustration is to be commended. Variety in the *sources* too. The element in preaching that is to oppose dullness and keep exposition fresh must not itself become stereotyped. When a man is illustrating from a subject of which he is a master, he will move with most ease, because he is certain of the facts and has the confidence that properly belongs to a man speaking in his own province. But when he draws an analogy from a sphere or calling he does not fully understand, let him confirm the details from someone whose province it is, lest he provoke the remark heard in Liverpool after a distinguished divine had preached a special sermon, and drawn an illustration from seamanship. A man who had taken ships from the Mersey to the Plate for half a lifetime remarked when worship was over, " That man might be a great preacher, but he'd be a mighty poor sailor." Palpable ignorance on subjects from which one chooses to take illustrations will undermine the confidence of one's hearers concerning things infinitely more important than illustrations. And, in this matter of illustration, it is not really hard to find the facts.

Yet, whatever a man's particular hobby may be, there is surely special interest and value for the preacher in seeing all that he can of how other people *work*. Many laymen suspect that a minister already lives a life strangely detached from the " rough-and-tumble " of their existence. One way to narrow the gulf that divides minister and people is for the minister to see people as often as he can at work, to get as close to an understanding of their conditions as is humanly possible, and take a keen and personal interest in their day-to-day lives.

And again, as a pleasing by-product, the illustrations present themselves and one has only to pick them up.

I remember the fascination of the Potteries, and the score of fine, fresh illustrations I found there — not just the obvious ones like the potter's wheel and its concomitants (though how good Jeremiah's image was I never knew till then) but what gold looks like before it goes into the fire, how the diseases that long shadowed this industry are being combated, how to pack an oven, what skill there is in firing. What superb artists this calling has in fee!

Crewe comes to my mind and its great railway works: immense locomotives swinging off the ground while men continued to work on them; the crane under the roof, which, at an " upward glance," seemed to bring whatever men needed. I remember the manufacture of rails, signal boxes, and all the impedimenta of a vast transport system. I remember also the three skillful craftsmen working quietly in their own department on artificial limbs.

" Isn't that a good hand, sir? Look, the fingers move! With a glove on, it would look quite normal." I turned that to good use. The guide had said on the early part of my tour:

" We have a railway system as near to perfect, I think, as any that has been devised . . ."

Really?

Yet those craftsmen, serving one company only, were working all day and every day on artificial limbs!

Nor will I ever forget my visit to a coal mine: the long walk half bent from shaft to coal face; the gloom, the dust, the sweat . . . the accident. I have watched the statistics of accidents in coal mines ever since. Coal is never cheap.

The mills I remember — cotton, woolen, and artificial silk. The jam factory, the tannery, the home of copper tubes, the asbestos works, the chocolate and cocoa makers . . . and fifty others.

Behind everything else, the tilling of the good earth and all the wise husbandry of the fields. How varied it is! The amazingly fertile fields of south Lincolnshire, the wide chalk farms of the Yorkshire wolds, the strange agriculture of the great Moss at Tarleton . . . and illustrations everywhere. Indeed, there are so many that, like the angler, you can " throw the little ones back." A touch of the fastidious grows with growing sensitivity in illustrations, and, as one's store enlarges, there must be " something really special " in everything one keeps.

3. *The Newspaper*

There is something more than a little inconsistent in the popular attitude to the newspapers. They are widely criticized — and widely read! People speak with hearty disparagement of them — and buy them just the same. Only the odd man here and there follows up his disapproval by cutting them completely out. A larger number sit over the sheets for forty minutes and then remark, " There's nothing in the paper today " (!).

Newspapers vary, of course. Some are at obvious pains to observe C. P. Scott's maxim, " Comment is free, but facts are sacred," and some are as obviously careless of it. It was of this latter group that Ramsay MacDonald said:

" We could pass laws and edicts, we could hamper them, we could give you the right to sue a newspaper that has got a falsehood prominently displayed for having sold itself under false pretenses, but nothing of that kind can be done without limiting liberty to such an extent that I will not do it.

" If this goes on unbridled and unchanged, I am perfectly certain the knowledge and judgment of our people will be so degraded that they will not be able to carry on their democratic responsibilities."

No man should choose his paper carelessly. Nor should he let his politics decide the issue for him. If the news service is really dependable, he can do his own independent thinking. The last thing a man should buy in a newspaper is an opinion.

Having chosen his paper carefully, let him look upon it as a page of history. Trenchant, sweeping, and utterly scornful comments on the press, which are not uncommon among men of scholarly attainment, reveal one of the defects of the academic mind. Newspapers *are* pages of history. A man known to be a master of the period, say, of Antiochus Epiphanes, or Ramesses II, or Stephen and Matilda, and who openly proclaims that he never reads a newspaper (and proclaims it just as loudly in his comments on current affairs), is plainly out of touch with life. Broadcast news is too swift, and too incomplete, to be a substitute. What immense events filled the best of the papers through all the twenty years of uneasy truce between the two world wars! What immense events fill them still! A man who takes a paper that never discusses such problems as: " Should girls use lipstick? Is it the red peril? " and never raises such questions as, " How can you give your nails glamour? " and which never employs that parasite of journalism, a " social gossip " man, but honestly offers the news and its own comments, should treat his paper with respect and learn to read events with discernment and inwardness. He is reading history. If he is a believer in God, he will be seeking God's purpose in the broad sweep of it. If he is a preacher, he has a harvest of facts brought to his door, and a wealth of illustration as well.

Most of us are busy men. Only a little time a day can be given to the newspaper. Ministers have been advised to read their paper standing, and to put it down when they are tired.[23] It prevents a man from giving time to the paper which should be given to the Bible, to his devotions, and to deeper thought.

Howsoever a busy man acts about that — sitting or standing — it is only a little time that he can give to the press. He knows what he wants. His particular journal may offer an itemized summary of the day's news down which he can run his eye in a moment, but, whether it

[23] John A. Hutton, *That the Ministry Be Not Blamed*, p. 171.

does or not, he knows his way about his own paper. The
social and stock exchange news may interest him only
slightly; racing and the reports of company meetings
hardly at all. But he moves quickly to the columns
where he will find what he wants, and soon the events
at home and abroad have passed under his swift eye. He
reads always with a heavy marking pencil in his hand.
As a preacher, the selective principle latent in his mind
is the triumph of righteousness in the world of men. The
things he marks might seem oddly assorted to someone
else: Divorce statistics. The profits of brewery com-
panies. A stipendiary's comments on the effect of " fun
lands " on juvenile delinquency. A summary of a Royal
Commission on housing. The will of a " turf account-
ant." A film review. A speech by an Indian leader on
Christian missions in his country. The dramatic critic's
comments on the " broad humor " of a vaudeville show
(pretty " broad " he thinks when the paper mentions
it!). The word under which he wants them filed he
plainly marks on each. All are soon cut out — or left to
some other member of the household to cut out for him.

One or two other things he marks also — not so easily
classified. He puts them apart from the rest.

Later in the day he broods over them. There is an
analogy hidden somewhere in these. He is questioning
them. " What ' other thing ' are you saying to me? " A
flicker of a smile at his lips registers a clear answer to his
question. " So that was it." These are not filed with the
rest. He has a special place for these. When their hour
comes, polished and fitted in their place, they will make
the truth laid on his heart clear to the people to whom
he is called to preach.

And here is a case in point. The sermon raised the

question whether or not life confirms the Bible teaching
that the way of transgressors is hard, and the statement
was categorically made that sin has a way of coming
home. It went on:

" A few months ago *The Times* reported a strange case of
crime in a certain German town. A lady in that town found a
basket on her doorstep, and the basket contained a pigeon.
There was a note also inside, an urgent, imperative, threaten-
ing note which said that if the lady did not fasten a certain
sum of paper money to the clip on the pigeon's leg and re-
lease the bird immediately, her house would be burned down
that night. The lady immediately informed the police and the
police acted with amazing rapidity for the detection of the
criminals. They chartered two airplanes and, having tied a
streaming ribbon to the bird's neck, they released the bird and
instructed the pilots to pursue it. The pigeon rose in the air
and wheeled round several times before it finally took its
course. The inhabitants of the town, who knew nothing, of
course, of the crime, stood in amazement at the strange gyra-
tions of the two airplanes and feared for their church steeple;
but as soon as the pigeon flew on a direct course the airplanes
were in hot pursuit, while the police followed, as best they
could, in a high-powered car below. Presently the pigeon flew
down to a loft and one of the airplanes took a photograph of
the spot, while the other dropped a note to the police. The
police dashed to the house and discovered two brothers unty-
ing the telltale ribbon in feverish haste from the bird's neck,
and they were placed under immediate arrest. The men, however, protested that the bird was not theirs. ' It just flew into
our loft,' they said; ' it is not our bird.' ' Very well,' said the
officer, ' we will test that,' and he ordered the pigeon to be
taken away and released from a distant spot — and it came
home. A second time it was taken away and a second time it
came home. A third time — and a third time it came home.
And every time it came home it deepened the certitude of
their guilt. Finally, they broke down and confessed. Their sin
had come home. Sin is like that. It comes home. It is mysteri-

ously in its nature to come home. Of yourself, you cannot kill it. If it does not come out, it comes up! "

Or consider the following: God's graciousness and wisdom in bringing good out of evil and making even our punishment yield a gain was under consideration, and the point was sharpened by this illustration which had its source in a few lines from the paper:

" A curious thing happened in South Africa recently. An old native woman, who had committed some trifling offense, was hauled before the courts and fined ten shillings. She protested her innocence, but finally burrowed in her garments and produced a golden sovereign, whereupon the clerk, making a reference to the present value of the coin and finding it to be thirty-two and six, collected the ten shillings and gave the old woman twenty-two and six change. The poor old soul, who knew nothing about the gold standard, left the court with her mind in a whirl. She must be feeling with Sam Weller that the law is an ass. Back home in her village she has been asking her friends how she could possibly be condemned for a crime and yet be paid a dividend upon it."

Ripped from its context, no illustration looks its best, but a connoisseur, picking up what appears to be a trifle, can always see it, in his mind's eye, polished and set. No doubt the newspaper reference to the herd of cattle being driven over a wooden bridge, which Dr. Watkinson turned into so effective an illustration (pp. 28 f.), would have seemed an unimportant trifle to the mass of folk running their eye over the page. One can almost guess the telescoped heading of the two or three lines: " Cattle Scared Crossing Bridge." But on the sensitized mind of Dr. Watkinson it registered immediately. He may not have seen its analogical use at once, but he would have respected the intuition which said, " There's something here." There was! His hearers knew it when he riveted their attention and, by the aid of that unconsidered trifle, made the truth to live.

One does not read the newspapers for illustrations but for news. Yet — as we have found elsewhere — the illustrations are there.

4. *General Reading*

It seems to be generally established now that it is not a good thing to label certain books as " classics " and insist that every educated person ought to read them if, in point of fact, you want to get them read. Allowing for the eagerness with which the ill-read seek to excuse themselves on the ground that they were wrongly taught, it is hard to resist the weight of evidence that has been heaped together to show that Shakespeare, or Milton, or Jane Austen was " spoiled " for a large number of people at school. A skillful teacher of English today comes to his task with more cunning. If he cannot say without qualification, " Follow your own taste: read what you like," he gets as near to it as he can, while cleverly refining that difficult sense of taste.

Preachers, when they are not concentrating on their direct preparation for a pulpit, have as much liberty as anybody else to read what they like. The question which our inquiry raises for us is this: " Reading what he likes, is it possible that he will derive something more than mere enjoyment? Should he be alert for illustrations here as well? "

He certainly should. Most reading without a pencil at hand is wasteful. Enjoyment can be heightened, not lessened, by note-taking.

It is a common mistake to confuse reading and thinking. The profoundest thinkers I have known were not great readers. Some thinkers are great readers, of course, but the point to notice is that they need not be. Time can be wasted as easily with books as with bridge, and *how* you read is as important as *what* you read.

One of the compliments that ignorance pays to a little culture is to assume that any man reading anything other than the lightest of light novels is " studying." A preacher is often flattered by hearing that assumption in the simpler members of his congregation. Many a minister who has misused his morning with someone's entertaining memoirs, or one of these gossipy literary concoctions which publishers evidently find lucrative, and which deceives a man into believing that he is more widely read than he really is, must have felt at least half ashamed when his wife inquires at lunch if he has had a *very* hard morning of study. In his heart of hearts he knows that those morning hours, fenced with difficulty from unnecessary distractions, are his for the hardest thinking and hardest praying of his day.

Yet, even when the hours of legitimately lighter reading come, he need not waste his time. Let him read, with a pencil in his hand, sensitive to the possibility of illustrations; marking and claiming whatever his developing judgment tells him will have some future use.

(a) Biography

Most people have heard by now of the temperance enthusiast who, urging a man who had been imbibing too freely to sign the pledge, spoke about the badness of beer.

The poor soaker was roused to a protest. He fixed the reformer with a watery eye and said, as firmly as his hiccuping would allow:

" No, sir. There's no bad beer. Some's better than others."

I have sometimes felt like that about biographies. There are no bad biographies. Some are better than others.

I exaggerate, of course. There *are* bad biographies. But not many. And when one has learned to smell out the jaundiced judgment and skip the tedious panegyric, there are not many biographies — or autobiographies — that have not something to give.

If we are right that nothing illustrates life like life, it need not to be argued that biography is a deep and rich mine. The preacher who finds his light reading (or much of it) in biography soon has a mass of pertinent material on call. Saints and sinners, soldiers and statesmen, writers and philosophers — it is all a thick vein. If, in the last resort, the preacher is commending a way of life to the people, how can he better illustrate the character of it than by showing what were the practical consequences in specific lives of counsel heeded or counsel ignored?

(b) Travel, Science, and Natural History

We have agreed that in his lighter moments a preacher may read what he likes, and we have agreed also that a man is likely to illustrate with more skill and safety when he is following his own bent and moving in a sphere that he has largely made his own. It is not without interest, however, to point out how wide is the sphere of analogical illustrations that may be drawn from books of travel, from science, and from natural history as well. Where genuine interest and enjoyment beckon a man on, it is amazing how rich is the yield. Some of the trifles one picks up may not seem (baldly stated and unrelated to the theme) treasure trove at all, but, coming at the right moment and in the right place, a small thing can fix a great truth in a hearer's mind.

Imagine the preacher to be speaking about the importance of environment and how guarded a Christian must be concerning the degree of its influence upon him. He wants to put that fact plainly to the people and he wants it to stay. He says:

" If you are wholly the product of your environment, a change in your environment will mean a change in you. One of the most curious birds known to ornithologists is the kea of New Zealand. It is, I believe, unique among birds in that its ancient habits were changed in the space of a few years by a change in its environment. The circumstances were these: The kea had fed from time immemorial upon the natural fruits, seeds, and insect grubs of the beautiful land in which it lived, and was known as a picturesque and harmless bird of the poll parrot type. But when the British settlers came to New Zealand and began sheep-rearing, the change in the environment of the bird produced an extraordinary change in the bird's nature. The kea took to haunting the sheep stations and feeding on the offal of those killed for consumption, and in course of time, it developed so strong a taste for the kidney fat that it became a vicious bird of prey, attacking the live animal, tearing open its side, and literally dragging the succulent morsel from the living carcass of the beast. That bird is now shot at sight. The poll parrot has become a vulture. Why? Because of a change in its environment — that is all; and there are some ' highly respectable ' people who would not survive a change in their environment and would as surely be swept to the cesspools if the current of life set that way."

Or, suppose that he is most concerned with the life of prayer and wants to show how, by its aid, a Christian can maintain a healthy spiritual life in an alien environment. He might make his point with an illustration drawn from natural history.

" There is a little water spider to be found in our ponds and ditches, who lives beneath the water's surface in a kind of diver's bell.

" This is how he does it: He makes a thimble-shaped case of silk which he anchors by fine threads to the water weeds at the bottom of the pond. The orifice is turned downward. The spider then goes up to the surface and, by means of hooked hairs which cover the lower part of his body, he entangles (as it were) a little bubble of air which he carries down and releases inside his little home. The air rises to the top of the bell that he has made and displaces a certain amount of water, and immediately he goes up again for more air and liberates it in the same way. Up and down he goes until finally the bell is filled with air and he lives, beneath the water's surface, something of the life above. As his use exhausts the oxygen he goes up for more, and he maintains his life in an alien environment only by a ceaseless vigilance.

" There is a lesson here for us. The life of the spirit can be properly maintained only by a constant correspondence with the spiritual world."

Or, suppose that he is grappling with the dark mystery of life and seeking to explain the ministry which pain and frustration can have in a world ruled by a God of love. The natural history of the Antipodes serves his purpose again.

" New Zealand is a fascinating country to those who are interested in geography and travel. Do you know that there are no dangerous wild animals and no dangerous reptiles native to New Zealand at all? Not one! Apart from its human occupants a child could have wandered through its primeval forests unharmed. Do you know also that New Zealand is the home of more flightless birds than any other country — the kiwi, the kakapo, the penguin, and the weka rail? These birds had wings but lost them by neglecting their use. Scholars

say they neglected them because food was always abundant
and there was no danger near — no fearsome beast or reptile.
And the cost of their immunity was the power of their wings.
They had no necessity to fly; now they have no ability to fly.
My friends, it would have been the same with us. The dangers we dread compel us to expand the wings of the spirit. It
is our need which drives us to the bosom of our God."

And there are millions more of these illustrations still
unclaimed. Occasionally, it is not possible for a preacher
to speak with definiteness on the facts which his illustration involves because the experts themselves have not
made up their minds. He need not worry overmuch. A
hint that the point is still disputed — and a modest
deference to the scholars in another realm (" Some experts believe . . .") — is all that is called for. So far
as the preacher is concerned, the illustration comes to its
homiletical end when it has conveyed the spiritual meaning he has in mind.

As for science, it is an unfathomable mine of illustrations. It has its own peculiar dangers for the preacher.
To most men in the pulpit it is an unfamiliar world, and
there are plenty of young people in the pews with spe-
cialist training on some subsection of science. Their crit-
ical minds can easily be estranged by a preacher's slip.
A man should be doubly sure, therefore, of his facts or
wisely " covered " by the name of a scientist of repute.

Scientific illustrations are also liable to be very involved. If the point is not easy to see, the illustration had
better be changed. That which is used to explain must
not itself require long explanation.

Nevertheless, when this seam is worked by a master,
it has the richest things to give. An age of science warms
to scientific allusion. It is a good thing that the men who

can do it well make free use of this means of illustration if only to let it be known that science and religion are not alien realms, though they will not, of course, be " reconciled " by sermon illustrations. The contributions of the ablest men to that high task will be the fruit of their flintiest thinking. But even sermon illustrations can show that the servant of the Word is a student of the world — and, if he does it with skill and obvious knowledge, the science students in his congregation will be especially grateful.

(c) Fiction

It is a rule with many busy ministers who have very little time to read fiction — and perhaps very little taste as well — to read two or three of the most significant novels a year. It is a wise rule. One *must* know what the people are reading and, if the books are wisely chosen, a man can keep in touch with the trends in literature that way.

They may not be best sellers. The book that " everybody is talking about " his wife will probably read, and she can tell him the tale. It is amazing what time an intelligent woman can save a busy man in that way. Her summary, and a few questions from him are usually enough. He can keep in the conversation on social occasions largely by her aid.

No! Let him ask a discerning friend whose business it is to watch books, or let him consult the ablest reviewers, and he will soon learn what fiction it would be well to read.

What use has *this* reading for sermon illustration?

Not, I think, a *great* deal.

When a man tries to take illustrations from novels,

he is wrong in assuming (even with the best sellers) that everybody has read them. When he begins, therefore, " You all know . . ." the plain fact is that they do *not* all know; and if he takes the line of assuming that the story must be explained for the sake of those who have not read it, he consumes more time than an illustration can normally be allowed.

If a man feels drawn to illustrate in this way, let him at least measure himself against the difficulties. It is *fiction*. Could he not make the point as well from biography and, therefore, from fact?

Is the incident he is selecting capable of swift presentation? Can he get the " atmosphere " and the point in a few strokes?

Yet the thing has been done well. Preachers have often taken illustrations from George Eliot, for example, with her intense (and not unnatural!) preoccupation with moral issues. The influence of a child on a soured man can be briefly but strongly drawn in *Silas Marner*. The haunting phrase on the last page of *Adam Bede*, " There's a sort of wrong that can never be made up for," will bring another illustration from the same pen swift to the mind of those familiar with her works.

5. *Pastoral Work*

Some well-known preachers never undertook pastoral visitation. Dr. J. H. Jowett, for instance. The peculiar difficulties of men who minister in a central church to a widely scattered congregation are not easily overcome on the pastoral side. It is hard to see how a minister in those circumstances could possibly go from door to door. Probably the only answer to the problem for a man in that position is to allot specific hours when he is available at the church for pastoral appointments, and encourage his people to travel to him.

But this is certain: There must be at least some loss to preaching if the preacher is not in pastoral touch with his people. It is not the worst definition of preaching to say that it is " the minister's effort to answer on Sundays the questions his people have been asking him in the week."

Pastoral contact with the people — howsoever undertaken — is a rich source of sermon illustration. It need hardly be said that no man would betray in public the intimacies of private conversation, but a man alert for illustration sees things and hears things that have valuable homiletic use and include no disclosure of confidences at all.

There is a special merit in *homely* illustrations. Congregations are composed mostly of busy people, tired in their toil for the bread of this life, and wounded, perhaps, as well as tired. Abstruse and ingenious illustrations cannot help them all. Literary and historical allusions remind many people of their own lack of culture and feed their inferiority. A homely illustration well drawn can help all.

The homely (in the English sense) is not the vulgar, or the crude, or the low. It is just " the homely." People who are so " refined " that they dislike the homely should be deliberately disregarded. They are " overnice "!

There is often a touch of humor in the homely illustration. It is no worse for that. A man who thinks that it is a sin for the pulpit to provoke a ripple of natural mirth is just as mistaken in his way as the man who demeans the pulpit by telling a funny story, just because it *is* a funny story, without pith or relevant illustrative meaning at all. If a man steers clear of both those horrible extremes, he will not run aground.

The quaint remarks of children, heard on his pastoral visitation, often give the minister something he can use for others. Dr. Henry Howard, sitting one day in the home of a poor family in his church, watched a little boy putting his waistcoat on. He put the first button in the third hole, and as he continued laboriously at his task, the minister drew his attention to the mistake.

" Oh, it's all right, sir," said the little fellow. " It will all come right in the end."

A trifling thing!

But who that heard Dr. Henry Howard, years after, speaking with smashing force of those shallow optimists who ignore ugly facts, turn a blind eye to the writing on the wall, and then blandly assure us that " all will come right in the end," can forget his masterly use of that deliciously absurd incident, or fail to recall the picture of the mystified little boy with two buttons over and no holes to put them in? If they are quite short, a *couple* of illustrations making the same point, but contrasted in type, drive the stake well home. A Biblical illustration and a modern homely one pair well. The preacher can turn to the development of his argument feeling that " so far " things are well tied up.

Sometimes — but not too frequently — the preacher can illustrate from his own home. Here is an instance: The sermon was examining the difference between convictions and opinions, and, in the progress of the argument, the fact was faced that people often cling with pathetic earnestness to cults and shallow little heresies with an intensity of conviction worthy of a better cause.

The plea, therefore, at this point of the exposition ran like this: " Be fixed — but be fixed to the things that are fixed! Hold fast — but hold fast to the truth! " It went on:

" When we were wed, my wife and I received a number of presents and, among them, a household wants indicator. I had never seen one before. It was a sheet of tin with lists of everything that should be in the pantry and larder, and beside each name there was a little pointer that could be turned. The idea was this: When tea was running low, you put the pointer round and that meant, ' We want tea '; if it was sugar, you did the same, and, at the end of the week, it was simple to read the indicator; the grocer's list was made in a moment, and housekeeping became (in theory) a matter of minutes. In the joy of our first homemaking, I recall my wife carrying the indicator to the kitchen and fixing it with her own hands to the inside of the pantry door.

" ' That is the best place,' she said. ' I shall be standing here when I realize our wants.'

" She forgot one thing. It was fixed to something that was not fixed. She turned the pointer to register our need for coffee, swung the door behind her, and all the little pointers went flipperty-flop. At the end of the week our condition was desperate. The indicator said, ' No tea,' but the caddy was half full. The indicator said, ' Plenty of sugar,' but we could not find a cube. We began to realize the seriousness of housekeeping!

" Then it was that I stepped in with masculine superiority and said: ' This thing must be fixed to something fixed. It will never serve our need until it is.' I nailed it to the wall.

" Be fixed on the things that are fixed. Hold fast the centralities of the faith. The gospel is not the invention of last week; it is the message once delivered to the saints."

Clearly, then, there are many, many fields of illustrations and they are white unto harvest. Is it true, also, that the laborers are few?

IV

On Call

DR. W. L. WATKINSON was once asked how he kept his
sermon illustrations, and he is reported to have answered,
" I remember them."

And no doubt he did. Or *some* of them. It is amazing
how a good natural memory, aided by a deep interest in
these matters, can summon suitable illustrative material
just as the need comes.

But it is plainly impossible for any man to remember all that he has gathered, unless he is in the pitiful and
unpardonable position of using about a dozen illustrations over and over again. A congregation subjected to
these weary repetitions can remember them as well as
the man who employs them. His people make their way
to worship, wondering, as they go, which of the favored
dozen it will be this morning.

The problem arises for the real craftsman (who would
scorn to " lift " illustrations from other preachers),
who, with patient assiduity, has been shaping and finding his illustrations through the years, and who cannot
reasonably expect the most excellent memory to recall
that the exact illustration for the point now to be made
was in a book he read five years ago. Some system he
must have. What should the system be?

The advice given to many students is to keep a " commonplace book " — a notebook of treasured findings. " Write down," they are told, " whatever strikes you in your reading, and it will be under your hand when the hour comes."

It should be noticed, in passing, that even this way of dealing with illustrations requires some kind of indexing. A commonplace book crammed with unclassified matter is no better than a bin. I remember calling on a minister late one Saturday evening and finding him feverishly turning over the pages of a commonplace book, which had run into several volumes, but, for all his turning the pages backward and forward, he could not find what he sought.

" There's a grand illustration here somewhere," he sighed finally. " I need it for my sermon in the morning, but I can't find it! "

When so much is said in praise of commonplace books, it may seem a little captious to speak against them — and it must be admitted that no man concerned with illustrations can cut them out. But he should resolve to limit their use as much as possible. The sheer, time-devouring labor of copying out long pages of matter that may, and may not, be useful, is enough to intimidate the boldest, and explains why many commonplace books never become stout volumes.

If a man is tearing the heart from an important theological book, and finds it best to make a précis of the whole — well, that is hard, mental work, and he expects to moil at it. But the kind of thing that goes into a commonplace book (stray thoughts, illustrative instances, possible analogies) — what hours of sheer labor the copying out represents. Is it the best use of the time?

Can a man who lives with the conviction that *all* his time is God's, and that even his recreation is not so much time kept for himself as time given by Christ, who has the right to *all* his time — can such a man not devise a better use of his Master's time and do more at less cost?

I think he can. Let him keep the commonplace book for the things that we have classified under "Observation" (the suggestive trifles picked up on his travels), and let him note here also the useful things heard in his visitation, and which we have set down under "Pastoral Work," but let him resolve that he will save unnumbered hours, at the very place where commonplace books usually waste them, by garnering the fine fruits of his general reading without laboriously copying out from borrowed books the things that pull his eager eye.

To begin with, he should possess the books he reads. Libraries are indispensable for *referring* to books, but they can be a snare so far as *reading* them is concerned. They have militated against the habit of each man making a modest library of his own.

Time is our most valued commodity, and it is one of the few things commonly counted precious which is shared out equally to all. We do not all live as long as one another, but there are just twenty-four hours in each day for the rich man in his castle and the poor man at his gate. While you are reading *this* you cannot read *that*. How important is the choice, therefore, of the books you read. How necessary to be sure beforehand that this book is worth the *time* it will take — more valuable by far than the shillings it may cost!

It is foolish to say that people cannot afford to possess the books they read. Let a man get deliverance from the itch to read the latest: let him assure himself (whatever the reviews say) that if that book is so good, it will keep; let him remember that some of the finest books of biography and autobiography, of travel and science, of natural history and classic fiction, can be picked up secondhand for coppers; and let him make a rule, which admits of few exceptions, that so far as reading is concerned (as distinguished from reference), he will concentrate on the books that he owns. As he grows in awareness of the fields that yield most to his husbandry, he will grow also in the art of picking up cheap the books he wants as sources of illustration.

And this will be just one of his great gains! He will soon realize that if there are twenty things in that good book which he would like to keep under his hand, those twenty things must needs be laboriously copied out if the book is borrowed, or else (as often happens, alas!) irretrievably lost.

But not a line need be written down if the book is his. The husbanding of time by that alone is immense. He could write a book himself in the hours thus easily saved.

Leave the commonplace book for choice things noticed and revealing things heard, and also for the few things taken from the rarely borrowed volume, but learn how to make a preacher's index of the many volumes you possess, and having chosen them wisely and read them closely, " possess " them in every sense of the word.

What do we mean by a " preacher's index "?

Many books have no index at all — which is a pity if the book really has something to say. Some books are best read through the index. If the book is devoted to a subject on which one is already creditably informed, a swift glance down the index is enough to enable a practiced reader to fix on the fresh contribution which this new writer brings.

But the index is not drawn from the viewpoint of a preacher. It is made — with varying degrees of ability — to facilitate reference to the volume once read, and invariably makes free use of proper names.

"Cowl, H. B.," may appear in the index and that, conceivably, is the key name to an incident in the book which is a compelling example of the grace of humility, but it is highly unlikely that a man, even with a good memory, is going to remember three years later that under the name of Cowl in such and such a book (to which he has not referred often in the meanwhile) he will find a telling illustration of the first of all the graces.

The books we read, and find fruitful for illustration, whether they have an index or not, must be provided, for our use and our own eye, with an index that makes them ready and eager to serve the supreme claims of the pulpit so that, when the foundations of the sermon are laid, and the general plan is in clear view, and the stout walls are beginning to rise, it may be easy, first to decide where the windows are necessary, and then swiftly to find them and put them in.

Here is a book taken at random from my shelves of biography: Ève Curie's life of her mother, *Madame Curie*.

And here, in my edition of the book, is part of p. 3 of the index:

Paderewski, Ignace, 98–9, 320
Painlevé, Paul, 110, 330
Paladino, Eusapia, 224
Paulsen, 189
Pellatt, Professor, 176
Poincaré, Lucien, 178

Who, glancing at this page of index a year after reading the book — " Sklodovska, Marie (Madame Curie), birth, 8; childhood, 8–15 " — would remember that p. 8 had brought them face to face with a remarkable and courageous Christian woman in Mme. Sklodovska, who loved her children as perhaps only good mothers do love, but who *never kissed them*. She was stricken with tuberculosis. It was her secret, and told to no one except by her " short attacks of dry coughing " and " a desolate shadow " on her husband's face. Marie grew up under an affection immense and tender, but an affection which had to strangle its normal expression for the sake of the children themselves.

Who would remember that " at school, 16–36," includes the story of Mme. Sklodovska's death, and the beginnings of granite agnosticism in the mind of the world's greatest woman scientist? Who could recall that " Paladino, Eusapia, 224," is a reference to the Curies' dabbling in spiritualism and raises the questions in the mind of the reader: " Is the hunger for religion in the heart of men and women ineradicable? " " If, by the bitter experiences of childhood, they reject the holy catholic faith, does the ache for the eternal demand a vent in other ways? "

The page is full of rich illustrative matter — but not

set out in a form easily recalled by a busy man even within a few months of reading the book. If the treasure is not to be lost, it must be made accessible under the themes a preacher's need would require.

Pencil in hand, and using the blank pages at the end of the book, the preacher might find himself, when he finished the volume, with part of his index something like this:

Not every man would make the same index. In the nature of things, one man would be struck by some incidents in the story and another by others but, with a latent sense of future homiletical needs, each man would make his own swift notes and, as the years went by, most of his reading would make its useful contribution to his store of illustrative material. There would be practically no wastage in his reading. He would not be haunted in after years by the thought of the hundreds of books he had poured through his brain, and which had soaked up the hours without leaving any valuable deposit that could easily be recalled. All his books would be awaiting his instant and ordered service. He would not be the sport of an erratic memory. He would not even be dependent on a good memory. Giving his best time every day to deep study and solid thinking, he would shape his sermon to the best of his ability and then squarely face the question how, by the aid of illustration, he could carry that hard truth into the core of his people's mind. Nor would he linger long in doubt. Both his memory and his notes would bring whatever he needed swift at his bidding, and he would have a mass of illustrative material all at hand.

A few further things must be said to make the method of indexing clear. A dot placed in the margin of the page saves time when turning up one's references. The eye is pulled to the relevant part of the page instantly, and one can determine at a glance whether or not it provides the illustration one needs.

There is, of course, no alphabetical order in the preacher's index as it appears when written at the end of the book. Its order has been determined, so far, entirely by the reaction of the reader's mind to the unfolding story.

This index must be " posted " to the preacher's chief index, which is in normal alphabetical order and receives the references from every book as it is read. It is the key to everything in a man's library — and more than his library. The contents of his commonplace book, carefully indexed, are " posted " here too — the things noticed in his travels and heard in his visitation. Always the key word for filing will be fixed without the needs of the next pressing sermon being allowed to " pull " the illustration away from the principle which it exactly illustrates. Being sure in his own mind in what segment of the message he will be working when that note is likely to serve his need, he will index it in such a fashion that, years after, his ordered and skillful references will ensure that at the right moment the telling illustration will present itself and say: " Here am I. Use me."

Nor must the useful gleanings from the newspapers

be overlooked here. These also have their link with a man's chief index. As a student of affairs and (in the sense in which every preacher ought to be) "a man of the world," the minister keeps his eye, as we have noticed, on facts concerning divorce, juvenile delinquency, drunkenness, housing, etc. — and all things that express the progress of the gospel in the life of the community. He is on his guard against the disposition to rave about " the world going to the devil " because two or three sad cases of immorality have come recently under his own eye. " What are the facts? " he asks. " What do the latest relevant statistics say? " A simple man with the facts under his hand can beat a great elemental thinker who has scorned to notice the relevant figures. Let him take these cuttings (their source and date on them) and file them in large envelopes labeled with the key word. Let him keep these envelopes in alphabetical order in a filing cabinet and make a reference under the same word in his chief index that there are pertinent news cuttings on the subject too.

Not so easily filed, but still more valuable in many ways, are the news cuttings turned (as we have seen) to analogical use. They can be slipped into an envelope and filed, or rather more obviously kept in a news-cuttings book, but must be carried in either case to the chief index to indicate that, on that theme, there are " cuttings " also.

No man will turn to these sources for the " stuff " of his sermons. God forbid! His Bible, his prayers, his best hours of hard thinking with God will provide that. He will never become a mere encyclopedist, fully informed as to what others have believed or said, but himself incapable of an original thought. He will not be content with the role of a " middleman," ever ready to hurry forward with other people's bright ideas, but strangely barren in them himself.

No! These stores are for illustration; at times, perhaps, for the stimulation of his mind; but never, never (while he retains mental self-respect) a substitute for his own searching in the Book of God, his own brooding, meditation, and prayer, or the beating out, on the anvil of his experience, the deep truth he has learned from Christ and life.

Such a man will never be caught building a sermon around his illustrations any more than a builder would (or could) build his house around the window frames. Stealing a couple of illustrations, and then looking for a text to hang them on, is the resort, he knows, of a man who has sadly missed his way. He asks forgiveness if there be any element of vanity in the resolution, but he is resolved to be a workman that needs not to be ashamed.

If a man uses a card index as the key to all he has, he can have it in strict alphabetical order, but, if he uses a book, strict alphabetical order is difficult because he is constantly adding new themes. He would be advised in that case to break up each letter in the alphabet into five columns according to which of the five vowels stands first in the word he is handling, and facility in reference can be quickened that way.

Some men catalogue their books, giving each of them a number, and any " postings " from the volume are simplified that way. The number of the book, followed by the number of the page on which the reference appears, is all that is necessary: e.g., 397/62. If a stu-

dent works with an interleaved Bible, and finds it easier
to relate his illustrations to texts rather than to subjects,
he can " post " his references direct to the Bible itself.
Or, if this kind of routine work does not fret him very
much, he could employ both methods, subject and tex-
tual too.

But systems of indexing vary and a man must find
out the methods which suit him best.

The method here suggested covers, in a simple way,
the five sources of illustrations which we have distinguished. A man can reach for what he wants in the
Bible by his memory and his concordance. The fruits of
his *Observation and Pastoral Work* will go into his commonplace book. The garnerings of his *General Reading*
will be gathered up by his preacher's indexes. The *Newspaper* yield will be filed in large envelopes and kept in
alphabetical order in a filing cabinet. The whole thing is
locked together in a central index which can be either a
book, or a set of loose cards, and is the key to all he has.

If it seems a little involved to explain, it is simple to
work. Nobody with office experience will need the explanation. Many of the tasks are routine and can be
delegated. A hard-working minister is not without people who are willing to save his time.

The extremes to avoid in indexing are, first, such a
lack of system that one cannot find quickly all that one
has on a given theme; secondly, such intricacy of system (with networks of cross references) that it takes
all one's time to keep the system going, and ceases to be
just a matter of moments in a busy man's day.

A system approximating to the system set out above
will have both simplicity and accessibility. It may seem

a lot of trouble to people who only preach to the same congregation occasionally, and who can rub along with what they borrow, or stumble on by accident. It will have no interest, either, for those who live on the sermons made for another congregation years ago. But men who face the same expectant people twice a Sunday, and for more than forty Sundays in the year; or who, though not under so great a demand as that, are determined to grind their own bit of corn — all these must work with method and order, and be quite certain that the good things they have gathered are all " on call."

V

Quotations: Prose and Verse

NOT all quotations in sermons are illustrations — not many are. They are called in usually to assist the argument more than to illustrate it, but because some of them are in the nature of illustrations, and because the broad question of quotations is related to our theme, it is important that we deal with it in this little volume, and it is convenient to deal with it now.

Some preachers make very free use of quotations — but not the greatest preachers. A sermon is distinct from a university thesis, or an academic examination of an old doctrine. Theological research, undertaken largely for scholars, invariably involves a man in extensive quotations. It is important that he make clear how his own contribution is related to that of his predecessors in this same field of study.

But preaching — the glad, clear proclamation of the grace of God to sinful men and women — is not to be confused with an academic thesis, or a treatise for the erudite. The preacher is commissioned to tell plain people in plain words the things that belong to their peace. It may be said quite definitely that no great sermon was ever a mosaic of quotations.

Quotations from the Bible are in a category by themselves. The Bible has an authority which no other volume can parallel or approach. The apposite, exact, and pertinent quotation of Scripture is a delight in any preacher but even here — if a man is careful to see that his quotations *are* apposite and pertinent to the particular theme he has in mind — they will not overweigh his own exposition of the text. It will be *his* message, given (with God's help) in *his* way, and, as succeeding stages in his theme are reached, an apt quotation from the Bible can hammer the truth home. But he must be sure that the citation is demanded. The Scriptures are not to be abused by loose and irrelevant quotation.

The difficulty arises in a more perplexing form when we deal with quotations other than those taken from the Bible. Power in preaching depends, in large part, on the ability of the preacher to make intimate and vital contact with every member of the congregation. He begins to do business with the people when, in the felt presence of God, he can lean over the pulpit and make each individual feel, " He is speaking to *me*." Quotations have a way of getting in between that " you and me " relationship. If they are so long that they have to be read, the very paper gets in the way as well. They are like intruders at a personal and private conference. Unless it is clearly important that they come in, they are best kept out.

Quotations, moreover, unless they are used with restraint, often leave the impression that a man has not been fully grasped by his subject. When a man is hot about his theme, and telling his hearers what it is most important and urgent that they should hear, he does not reach around for what other people have said, it pours out in his own words — improvable, no doubt, in grace of expression by a master of style — but, nevertheless, in clear and direct words which have the stamp of his own conviction upon them.

Consequently, we might frame this rule: *quote sparingly*. Use dictionaries of quotations only to confirm your own recollections and never to pick out a few gems of thought to stud your sermons. Catechize everything you are inclined to quote with stringency: " Do I need the help of that great name? " " Is that said so superbly well that I cannot hope to say it nearly as well in my own way? " " Does it impress me enough to remember it? Or is it so important that I *must* have it, even though I must have paper also to say what he said? "

It is not to be denied that to people with some width of reading there is a certain pleasure in literary allusiveness in preaching. Granted that the quotations are not too unfamiliar, need no introduction, and " swim " into a man's own style easily, they are picked up with delight.

Here are three examples taken from the same sermon.[24] The subject (based on John 4:35) was that " the youngest child, the most illiterate peasant, the most abandoned sinner, the most benighted pagan " has aptitude and hunger for religion. In different parts of the exposition we find this:

" Little children cannot understand theology, but they can enjoy religion. They do not understand entomology, yet they admire a butterfly; they know little of botany, yet they love the daisy; they are ignorant of optics, yet *their heart leaps up when they behold a rainbow in the sky*.

[24] W. L. Watkinson, *The Blind Spot*, pp. 86 f., 92, 96.

" We think of a skeptic as of something inhuman, but it is not so. His skepticism is not his deepest self. He has a religious self of which he cannot get rid by an intellectual decision. ' *Hath not a Jew eyes? Hath not a Jew hands, organs, dimensions, senses, affections, passions? Fed with the same food, hurt with the same weapons, subject to the same diseases, healed by the same means, warmed and cooled by the same winter and summer, as a Christian is? If you prick us, do we not bleed? if you tickle us, do we not laugh? if you poison us, do we not die? '* Is not the atheist also of the same flesh and blood? Hath not an atheist eyes to look out on this wondrous universe? Hath he not spiritual instincts and longings not easily denied, strange thoughts he cannot suppress, arguments within himself he cannot answer? Hath he not senses, passions, affections saturated with the supernatural? Whilst you sometimes doubt your belief, is not the atheist compelled to doubt his doubts?

" The New Testament represents the Church as a reaper, not as a sower; Christ is the Sower. He moves in his Spirit among the million, scattering living germs in the red furrows of human hearts, and the Church is to follow *reaping where it has not sown, gathering where it has not strawed.*"

We need not feel any objection to this. The sheer naturalness of it carries the thing through effectively and usefully. The only harm would arise in this kind of quoting if a man *strained* after it; left his hearers feeling that the " bits " had been fitted in and had the " joints " all showing; if he confused an essay with a sermon and blasphemously implied by his labored literary garnishings that preaching was a superior form of entertainment.

It is when a preacher is offering an opinion upon a subject that is likely to create controversy in the minds of his hearers that a pertinent quotation in his own support is most useful. Even then, to be fully effective, it needs to be quoted under a great name. The question has still to be argued, but clearly the matter has been well raised. The initial objection to the preacher's unusual opinion is countered by the proof that it is not his opinion alone. It was the opinion also, it seems, of Augustine, or Aquinas, or Calvin, or Law. Careful scrutiny is obviously called for.

Hardly less effective is the use of quotation when it is linked with the name of a man who, according to the common idea of him, would never have been expected to express himself in that particular way. Wesley's dependence on Luther is well known; Wesley's independence and criticism of Luther can still startle the uninformed. He said of Luther's commentary on the Epistle to the Galatians:

" I was utterly ashamed. How have I esteemed this book, only because I heard it so commended by others; or, at best, because I had read some excellent sentences occasionally quoted from it! But what shall I say, now I judge for myself, now I see with my own eyes? . . . How blasphemously does he speak of good works and of the law of God — constantly coupling the law with sin, death, hell, or the devil; and teaching that Christ delivers us from them all alike. Whereas it can no more be proved by Scripture that Christ delivers us from the law of God than that he delivers us from holiness or from heaven. Here (I apprehend) is the real spring of the grand error of the Moravians. They follow Luther, for better, for worse. Hence their ' No works; no law; no commandments.' " [25]

I remember the astonishment of a Lutheran pastor in Oxford brought face to face with that quotation. When he was made to see that it was not uttered in an un-

[25] *Journal,* II, p. 467.

guarded hour in Wesley's life, but was the natural expression of the mind of a man who much admired the
ante-Nicene Fathers, and who was never a slavish imita-
tor of his great predecessor in the Evangelical Succession,
it gave him a new understanding of one whom he fool-
ishly supposed might have been a Lutheran pastor himself.

In turning from prose quotations to verse, it is interesting to inquire if there is more to be said for quotations
in sermons from poetry than from prose, or vice versa.
My own opinion can be expressed quite simply. In
sermons — and sermons are not essays — poetic quotations should be used as sparingly as prose quotations,
especially when they run beyond two or three lines. I am
not including hymns in this counsel of restraint. Hymns
are in a different category, and perhaps the consideration of what distinguishes a hymn from what is normally regarded as great poetry would bring us swiftly to
the heart of what I have in mind.

The words of a hymn may, or may not, be regarded
as good poetry. They are usually expected to scan and
to rhyme, but sometimes they do not do that, and often,
from any high poetic standard, they do no more. Great
poets, even when they have been great Christians, have
never been great hymn writers.

In the hymnbook I know best, containing nearly one
thousand hymns, only seventeen of the authors have any
reputation as poets apart from hymnology, and less than
a third of this number would be placed in the front
rank. What constitutes a " great " poet is still a matter
of dispute and opinion, but less than forty of the one
thousand hymns come from the pens of men normally

classified as " major " poets, and who might be expected, therefore, to produce them. Whether the supreme figures in hymnology — and one in particular — should not be accorded a place among our great poets, for their contributions in this realm alone, is a provoking question which we must not pursue now.

Why are our great poets, even when they are convinced Christians, not among our great hymn writers?

The whole answer to that question would be a long one and not relevant to our main purpose. Some people would dismiss it abruptly by saying that few of our great poets were orthodox believers, and few had the spiritual discernment that the writing of hymns requires. But that is not the whole answer to the question. It is another part of the answer that is relevant now. Great poets are not normally simple and direct enough in expression. The poet, taking wing into realms of daring thought, outsoars the needs and natural expression of the majority of people who compose a typical congregation anywhere. In contriteness, and simplicity, and humility, the people come to church and to God and, when they say,

> " ' What language shall I borrow
> To thank Thee, dearest Friend? ' "

they are really reaching for language which — however much it soars in spiritual yearning — remains simple and swiftly understood.[26]

Most rich verse like most good music must make a " path " in the brain before full appreciation rises. Hearing it for the first time, one does not quite get it. By

[26] Cf. F. J. Gillman, *The Evolution of the English Hymn,* pp. 258, 269.

repetition it becomes familiar — with something more to give on every repetition — and slowly one claims the treasure as one's own.

When poetry is given to people in a sermon — poetry they may be hearing for the first time (however familiar it may be to the man who is quoting it) — it is fatal to the preacher's purpose if the people do not get it. At the best (in such circumstances) he has lost power and pace, and, at the worst, their minds go off at a tangent, and it may take a very cunning illustration to pull them back.

When a preacher is himself fond of verse, it is asking a great deal of him to resist the habit of frequent and fitting quotation (" You know that sonorous thing in Milton and that fine passage from Browning's ' Sordello ' . . .").

Nevertheless, he must be asked! At least, he must be urged to curb any tendency to do it often. He must question the quotation that leaps to his mind, and inquire whether its point can be swiftly grasped by people unused to poetry and hearing it for the first time; or whether it yielded its sweetness to him only by familiarity, and derived its power from subtle overtones requiring a keenness of ear to pick up. If the most cultured members of his congregation must not be forgotten — and, of course, they must not — the preacher must remember that life has not left much time for poetry to the majority of the people he faces and who have been so busy struggling for the bread of this life that they have not had much time for life's refinements. That is no reason why they should not hear good verse, wisely chosen, now and then, but preaching is an urgent and solemn business and (in the view of the writer) leaves little room for the merely decorative.

It would ill befit me to judge of the motives of other men, but when I have heard one graceful (and unusual) poetic quotation follow another — and another — all through a sermon, I have wondered whether it was a half-unconscious display of the width of a man's reading. I have thrust the thought from me as being an unworthy one, but what I could not thrust from me was the conviction that it impeded rather than quickened any movement of thought the sermon possessed, and left the irreverent youths in the congregation saying under their breath, " So what? "

Yet, there *are* sublime moments in preaching when the right poetic quotation can do what no prose can achieve. None who heard him forgot Alexander Whyte preaching on our Lord in the Garden, and especially his mention of the seamless robe:

" What a coat was that for which the soldiers cast their lots! It was without seam, but — all the niter and soap they could wash it with — the blood of the Garden and of the pillar was so marked upon it that it would not come out of it. What became, I wonder, of that ' dyed ' garment? and all that ' red apparel '?

" ' If you have tears, prepare to shed them now.
You all do know this mantle; I remember
The first time ever Cæsar put it on.
'Twas on a summer's evening, in his tent,
That day he overcame the Nervii.
Look, in this place ran Cassius' dagger through;
See what a rent the envious Casca made;
Through this the well-beloved Brutus stabb'd,
And as he pluck'd his cursed steel away,
Mark how the blood of Cæsar followed it, . . .
      Then burst his mighty heart;

And, in his mantle muffling up his face,
Even at the base of Pompey's statuë,
Which all the while ran blood, great Cæsar fell.
O, what a fall was there, my countrymen! . . .
Now let it work.'

" And as Peter preached on the day of Pentecost, he lifted
up the seamless robe he knew so well, and, spreading it out in
all its rents and all its blood spots, he charged his hearers, and
said, ' Him ye have taken, and by wicked hands have crucified
and slain.' " [27]

Notice that there was no introduction to this. Out it
came! daring, arresting, moving, and all the more power-
ful because most people have studied *Julius Cæsar* at
some time or other, and the quotation — without being
in any way hackneyed — had already its own " path "
in the brain.

Quotations from hymns avoid the difficulties we have
stressed in the deeper poetry. They are judged by the
right authorities of the Church to be the best *as hymns*:
they are simple, direct, and always, at least, vaguely
familiar. The apt quotation of a couplet from the hymnbook can be very telling as any preacher knows. He
might know something even better (for himself) in
Paradise Lost, but it will be counted as a virtue if he sets
aside what might be obscure to his hearers in favor of
a verse his people will grasp more eagerly, and the sub-
sequent singing of which will mean something that it
has not meant before.

The habit into which a few men get of *always* finish-
ing a sermon with a verse of a hymn is best broken. The
people know that he is breasting the tape when he spurts
to a rising inflection and begins to declaim the selected

[27] *Lord, Teach Us to Pray*, pp. 139 f.

verse. It would be well to break the habit if only because it *is* expected. " A new way is better than an old way even when it is only just as good."

It ought to be unnecessary to add that when a man quotes, he ought to quote with accuracy. But frequent public misquotations prove that the remainder is still called for. It irritates the people who know and (if frequently done) undermines their respect for the minister's mentality.

That is a risk which no preacher can afford to run.

VI

Mistakes Commonly Made

MORE than once during our study of the art of sermon illustration we have noticed in passing certain pitfalls that beset the feet of the unwary. It would be well if we glanced at some of them again, and then took the closest heed of others, still more important, which have not claimed our attention at all.

(*a*) We have rejected the idea that illustrations are ever legitimately used as decorations. We have not found it possible to reconcile the solemn, urgent business of proclaiming the grace of God to dying men and women with the practice of " decorating " what one has to say. At certain seaside resorts the effort is made by enterprising councils to make the promenade more attractive to visitors by lacing the trees and lamp standards with colored electric bulbs. They give only a minimum of light but they are thought to make the place more beautiful and to add to the gaiety of holiday crowds.

Illustrations in sermons should never be used like that. They are meant to be arc lamps. If they are beautiful in themselves, that is fortunate and pleasing, but their purpose is severely utilitarian. They are there to throw a flood of light upon the road. Consequently, no man will ever tell a tale in the pulpit for itself alone. Time enough for his gifts as a raconteur on less solemn occasions, but he is standing now between God and men, and however much he may be on guard against magnifying himself, he must never fail to magnify his office. No prophet was ever taken seriously who did not himself feel the awefulness of his calling. A dilettante in a pulpit is repugnant.

(*b*) We have rejected the idea also that a serious preacher will ever build his sermons *around* his illustrations. It is not improbable that, now and then, as a man broods on an illustration that has leaped upon him from life, that the truth it expresses will take firm hold on his mind and send him pondering to the Book of God. It is not unlikely that, as he thinks deeper and deeper upon it, some text or aspect of the subject will demand to be preached upon, and the illustration fall into its natural place. But any tendency to reverse that process must be resisted. The truth must grip him in itself and demand to be expressed; the illustration, if it can, will serve that major purpose.

(*c*) We have noticed also that illustrations which need explaining are hardly illustrations at all. A church is not a lecture hall, nor a pulpit a professorial chair. Time was when the clergy were the only teachers of the people on most subjects, and a case might have been made out in those ages for a wider latitude in general instruction than can be allowed in the pulpit now. If a man, in an effort to make the truth of God clear to people, chooses illustrations so obscure that they eat up his moments in explaining what they mean, he cannot possibly be regarded as making the best use of his time.

(*d*) Nor have we found it possible easily to excuse men who feel the importance of illustration and yet seem not to make an effort to achieve variety in it. The preacher who always illustrates from his own hobby, or favorite author, or particular academic or ecclesiastical interest, becomes a bore.

He is not less of a bore though his interest be the very highest, and though he undoubtedly carries specialized knowledge about it. The man who was once a missionary in Burma and cannot, alas! open his mouth in public on any aspect of the wide Christian gospel without getting back to Burma, would be shocked if he knew how much his regular hearers hate the sound of the place. The preacher who has been fortunate enough to make a tour of the Holy Land but is now, it seems, incapable of mentioning any place from Dan to Beersheba without telling the congregation (what they painfully know already!) that he has been there, is hardly better than a golf or angling bore. Indeed, he is worse! He makes *holy* things distasteful.

(*e*) Nor have we overlooked the peril of mixed metaphors. If figures of speech are illustrations in miniature, it is important to keep the picture clear, and the most practiced public speakers are all capable of a sideslip here. Indeed, it is easily possible to become pedantic about mixed metaphors and to forget that the English language is almost a graveyard of faded figures of speech. Most of us, for instance, use the word " undermine " as synonymous with " attack," and a man who examined our sermon to see if, having used the word " undermine " in the early part of the paragraph, we were careful to preserve the mining metaphor to the end, would be both a pedant and a pest.

That degree of finesse is not asked for, but glaring mixed metaphors we must avoid.

Even the greatest err here. Shakespeare said:

"O, I die, Horatio;
The potent poison quite o'er-crows my spirit." [28]

He said also:

"No, let the candied tongue lick absurd pomp,
And crook the pregnant hinges of the knee." [29]

It is impossible to feel that the keenest hearers at the Globe Theatre were not jolted by figures as strangely mixed as these, and to jolt people in this wrong way when one is trying to persuade them is foolish in a preacher and a playwright as well.

Something much more severe than a jolt, however, was administered to Sir James Sexton, "the dockers' M.P.," by the peroration of his chairman at a meeting Sir James had promised to address in the town of Hyde in Cheshire:

"Comrades, list to the clarion call! The plank of progress is now ripe for plucking. Soon shall we see the Socialist avalanche descending from the mountaintops and, with its mailed fist, crushing beneath its iron heel the ca-pit-a-list snake in the grass which is barring the progress of the floodgates of democracy from walking hand in hand with the British lion over the rich fields of prosperity from which we draw the sweet milk of iron, coal, and cotton." [30]

The power of that unhappy example will serve to re-mind us that illustrations — even in miniature — have their perils and none can ignore them with cheerfulness.

(*f*) If, to these other reminders, we add the danger already noted of looking upon preaching as a form of self-display, and seizing the fugitive moments in the

[28] *Hamlet*, v, 2.
[29] *Hamlet*, iii, 2.
[30] *Sir James Sexton: Agitator*, p. 172.

pulpit to demonstrate the width of our reading and learning, we shall be on our guard against all the more obvious dangers and can turn to the consideration of other perils that have not come under our survey in these pages so far.

1. *Don't confuse illustration and argument*

Such a dictum has only to be stated to win its willing reception into any ordered mind. Obviously, illustration and argument are not the same thing.

But they are often confused. The Greeks were aware of the danger, and not a few philosophers have commented on it since, notably Locke. The transposition is not difficult to make. Grant that a man is carried away by his subject, deceives himself first and is facing an uncritical congregation, and the damage is done before he is fully aware of what has happened. The illustration is accepted as the argument in his own mind, and in the minds of many of his hearers.

But not all! His keenest hearers will notice the substitution. If they are convinced that the preacher has deceived himself, they will judge him to be morally blameless only by losing respect for his reasoning powers.

It is a high price for a preacher to pay. Men with the best case in the world to set out should shudder at the thought of losing the respect of those who (in some ways) they are most eager to win.

2. *Don't make a rule that each sermon must contain a given number of illustrations, and don't illustrate the obvious*

If the subservient place of illustration is always borne in mind and if the preacher never forgets that its whole purpose is to illustrate the truth and carry it into his hearers' minds, he is not likely to forget that illustration is only demanded by what is obscure and possibly also by points that are quite unimpressive unless they are made to live by vivid incident.

Illustrating the obvious is a waste of time and a source of annoyance to a congregation.

It must be remembered, of course, that what is obvious to one person may not be obvious to others and obvious things are sometimes strangely overlooked. Congregations vary — and individuals vary within them. A preacher keeps his eye on the charwoman as well as on the schoolmaster.

But intelligent people are intelligent enough to realize when a man is gathering up the slower members of his flock with an illustration he knows to be necessary for them, and will wait not impatiently for the argument to proceed. It is when a man offers an illustration that nobody needs, and not only offers it but holds on to the puerile thing, that a congregation feels intellectually insulted.

I remember the wrath of a working woman who had listened to the curate preach. Padding out a point already plain (and not worth making in the first place, she thought), he had gone on to say:

" Now let me take an illustration from a pair of scales. . . . Now you all know what scales are. Scales are things we weigh with. . . ."

Her droll mimicry of the curate's unctuous manner and his fade-out voice remains with me still. So does her stinging scorn!

3. *Don't labor the moral*

We have laid it down as a rule that an illustration cannot be a good illustration if it needs to have its point labored. Even children have long since rebelled against sententious moralizing. They become restless the moment the unskillful speaker begins " applying " his tale.

We have pointed out that with the exceptions of the parable of the Sower, and the Wheat and the Tares, Jesus never applied his parables — and even then he did so only at the disciples' request.

He said, " He that hath ears to hear, let him hear." [31]

That was all! It was all there, if you had a modicum of spiritual discernment to take it: tale and truth together.

This is not to say that a man may not give the point of his illustration a couple of hammer strokes when he has made it. Indeed, he would be wise to do so. But only a half-wit would confuse that with moralizing and it should be done with clean, chiseled phrases which can be driven swiftly and sharply in.

Nor must it be forgotten that, however skillfully and earnestly the truth is presented and illustrated, there will be people so inattentive to what is said, or so limited in their apprehension, that they will not grasp the point so plainly made and even infer the precise opposite from what is intended. A friend of mine, preaching with great clarity and skill on the text, " Ephraim is joined to idols," [32] was startled, in being thanked afterward, to discover that he was being appreciated for the wrong

[31] Matt. 11:15.
[32] Hos. 4:17.

thing. " That's what I say," said the enthusiastic wor-
shiper. " Leave them with their idols. I never did believe
in foreign missions myself."

All preachers run that risk. Their aim must be, however, to reduce it to a minimum; to preach with such
plainness that even the slow of understanding are carried along and if, having done their utmost, they still
fail, it may comfort them to remember that the divine
Son of God did not always succeed in lodging the truth
in people's minds.

4. *Don't forget the facts*

It is one of the complaints of purists who object to
the use of anecdotes in preaching that so often the story
that is related is false, sometimes in whole and sometimes
in part. " It is almost a form of fable," they say. " It is
a piece of fiction made to serve a homiletical need but
told as though it were actually true."

Nor is this denied by all the preachers who employ
the anecdote. Some frankly make them up, treating
them almost as parables, and feeling no more guilt about
it than Dickens would have felt if he had been accused
of inventing the incidents set out in *Oliver Twist*.

Even among the men who would hesitate to invent
moral tales (*and tell them as if they were true*), it is not
unusual to " embroider " or " improve " a true story, to
say, not what the man said but what he ought to have
said, and to retouch the incident in such a way that in its
final form it bears only a dim resemblance to the facts.

What are we to say about these devices? Can they be
excused in men who claim to be ministers of the Word
of truth?

I do not think that they can be excused. One can allow a wide and legitimate margin to a man in the manner in which he relates an incident (and no small part of the storyteller's art lies here), but one must still insist with any preacher that he keep (so far as he knows them) to the facts. Few things tend to undermine the respect for the pulpit in the pew than the suspicion that the preacher is careless in his handling of truth.

If a man needs a picture to portray his point, and has no clear and factual instance that he can offer to the people, let him invent by all means — but let it be clear that it is the fruit of his imagination and makes no claim to relate something that actually occurred. The device is quite simple. Its invented character needs not to be labored. A simple prefatory phrase is enough: " I see it like this. Suppose . . ." Or, " I picture it to myself in this way." The people enter into the spirit of the illustration quite easily. Their minds march right on with the preacher. In the time of our Lord there was probably no risk of misunderstanding the nature of the parable. It seems that the invented story was common form with the rabbis then.

One of the commonest dishonesties in the pulpit and on the platform is the relation of an incident that happened to somebody else (if it ever happened at all) as though it happened to the speaker. The assumption, I suppose, which lies behind this deception, is that the point would lack pith unless it were told in the first person. But a man who does this often soon forfeits the respect of his hearers and occasionally exposes himself to a public humiliation as well. A few years ago, at a religious conference, a well-known preacher evoked a storm of laughter by telling a good story as illustrative of his point. The story was received even better than he expected. As the laughter rolled toward the platform, in wave after wave, his expression seemed to say, " Well, I knew that that was a good story, but I didn't think it was as good as that."

He was sublimely unaware that the same story had been told earlier in the evening by a speaker who had addressed the meeting before he, himself, had arrived, and who was sitting near him on the platform sharing his embarrassment at the prolonged mirth. Mr. A had told it of Mr. A; Mr. B had told it of Mr. B. The conclusion to which some of their questioners came afterward was that it had not happened to either of them. It is not possible to remain entirely at ease when you find an audience laughing at you and not at your story. People do not laugh aloud in church when a preacher errs in this way but something dies in them: all trust in the man who came ostensibly to show them the way to heaven.

We have already argued that the anecdote has its minor place in the pulpit, but the rule with anecdotes, as with all other illustrations that claim to have happened, is plainly this: keep to the facts.

5. *Don't glorify yourself*

All progress is progress in humility, and there are few spectacles more sad than that of a preacher unconsciously advertising in the pulpit his failure in this lovely grace.

It comes out in subtle ways. He may refer to a distinguished person whom he has met once or twice as " my friend." His manner of relating a story has a way of shedding light upon himself (more than he knows!!). " I was once addressing a *great* congregation in . . ." " In desperation, hardly knowing what to do, he turned to *me* . . ." " I was hurrying along, in an endeavor to keep *my rule of fifteen pastoral calls in an afternoon,* when . . ."

Just overtones! And all true, no doubt! But what chronic condition of vanity is it that casts statements into these molds and adds unnecessary words and clauses to set the self in a pleasing light?

Let the preacher be on his guard against this. Let him remember that it can grow on a man, and blind him as it grows, so that he is not only unaware of it himself but would even impute a nasty mind to those who notice the innuendos to regret them. Let him remember the wider implications of that deep word of James Denney: " You can't in preaching produce at the same time the impression that you are clever and that Christ is wonderful."

Our people are often more spiritually sensitive than we know. They have a fairly shrewd idea whether or not their minister is " thick with God." They notice the subtle self-display of such phrases as we have quoted above and which (when it is a feature of a man's preaching) they cannot help deploring. And they know also when their minister is nigh to being a saint and wears the robe of real humility (though always as an undergarment) and from him they will take the occasional full disclosures of his heart without any sense of impropriety and with no false inference concerning its purpose.

The people of Free St. George's knew the worth of Alexander Whyte. They knew too his humbling humility. They knew that he thought himself " the worst man in Edinburgh," and they knew his sincere belief

that if his people could see into his heart they would
" spit in his face."

When Alexander Whyte gave an illustration in which
he figured largely himself, nobody inwardly accused him
of self-glorification. His intense spirituality secured him
from that.

Hear him expounding, " And for their sakes I sanctify
myself." [33] Listen while he pleads with his people to in-
tercede for " some child or some other relation; some old
schoolfellow or college friend; some partner in business; or some companion in sin ":

" I cannot tell you the terrible shock a case of that kind
gave to myself last week. There is a man still in this life I had
neglected to pray for, for a long time past. Days and weeks —
and I never once mentioned his name. I used to sanctify myself for his sake, but daily self-denial is uphill work with me,
and I had insensibly slipped out of it. But, as God would have
it, a letter came into my hands last week that called back my
present text to my mind. I may not tell you all that was in
that letter, but the very postmark made my heart to stand
still. And as I opened the letter and read it — Shall I tell you
what I felt? I felt as if I had murdered my old friend. I felt
as if he had been drowned, while, all the time, I had refused
to throw him the rope that was in my hand. I felt his blood
burning like vitriol on my soul. And a voice cried after me
on the street, and would not be silent even in my sleep, ' Thou
art the man! ' I could get no rest till I had resolved, and had
begun to *sanctify myself* again unto importunate prayer for
his sake. To deny myself, to watch unto prayer, and to take
his name, night and day, back to God. ' I cannot let Thee
go unless thou dost save that man; if he is lost, how can my
name be found in thy Book? ' How I will persevere and succeed, in my future sanctification for his sake, I cannot tell.
The *event* alone will tell! At any rate, I have preached this

[33] John 17:19.

sermon this morning out of my own heartsore experience, as
well as out of this great intercessory text." [34]

But one must be " far-ben " (as the Scots would say)
to do that. Such a word only reverberates from beneath
the sounding board of a holy life. And when it does, it
is unforgettable.

6. *Don't neglect the setting of the illustration*

We have had frequent need in these pages to mention
the importance in illustrations of the " mount." It is,
indeed, nearly as important as the illustration itself.

There is usually an exact position for any particular
illustration in the development of a sermon. The position varies, of course, with the illustration and with the
sermon, but any man with a sense of sequence, and a
" feel " for an illustration, knows to a nicety where it
must come.

The illustration will have its full power only in that
position. Used too soon, it is half thrown away; deferred,
it arrives like a laggard, and is felt to be redundant.

If a man has no sense of time in regard to these things,
it would be hard to teach it, but a hint or two can be
given.

A sermon may begin with an illustration if the illustration pictures the problem, and brings it into quick
focus, for the early part of the sermon must be normally
concerned about that. It is *raising* the question. If the
sermon belongs to any of the sermonic forms that argue
a case, the case must be set out with some swiftness and
(if the sermon is to have balance) with such economy
of time that the preacher is not compelled to break off

[34] *Lord, Teach Us to Pray,* pp. 128 f.

when the problem has been clearly set out in all its awkwardness, but with no time left to clear it up.

The more natural and necessary place for the illustration is when the case is stated, and is proving perplexing, and when the honest preacher compels his hearers to look squarely at the God-denying look of things (as seen from this angle) and when the mental darkness thickens all around. " How do we get out of this? " is written all over the people's faces.

Now, let the preacher begin his answer. There is no *obvious* reply to a problem so deep. The cleanest, plainest, most-Saxon prose he can command is not equal to making his meaning clear to all his hearers while it remains pure exposition. He needs an illustration. While the perplexity is still deep but some glimmering apprehension of God's answer is beginning to appear, he reaches for the analogy he needs and the light shoots out like a single searchlight suddenly switched on in a pitch-black night. *This* is the position for the illustration. Here! Just here! Any light shines brighter " amid th' encircling gloom." The ugly facts have been faced — and outfaced! Gleaming in that analogy is the answer. Preacher and congregation move forward together.

When the moment has come for the illustration, *give it.* To parley then is to lose pace. To give notice that you are going to illustrate is foolish. Turn the light on!

Who has not heard a wearisome preacher ambling forward with phrases like these? " I heard the other day of a story that I think might illustrate this point, and which I would now like to pass on to you. You may judge yourself whether or not it does, indeed, illustrate what I want to say . . ."

Bah! He is nearly as boring as Thackeray who, in

some of his books, can hardly get a character on the way without explaining why he chose this character and not that! [35] Leave such fumbling to the novelist, if he cannot take firmer grip of his work than that, but let the preacher move forward without breathlessness but with deliberate speed. Half an hour to wake the dead! The urgency and overwhelming importance of it all must make him, like King Alfred, a " noble miser of his time " from whom unnecessary patter " no moment steals."

All the preface a normal illustration requires is this: " *Let me illustrate!* " Be glad when it does not even require that.

7. *Don't use illustrations that steal attention from the sermon theme*

Odd as it may seem, some illustrations — some good illustrations — must be jettisoned by any man who would be a master of this craft.

It is possible for an illustration to be too interesting, and too interesting *in itself*. The perfect illustration does its work, and exhausts itself in so doing. The thought of the congregation is concentrated on the sermon theme. The illustration is merely a lamppost. One does not want to embrace it, or study it as a work of art. One is grateful for the light it sheds, and travels on.

If an illustration almost compels interest in side issues, and leaves the congregation dawdling on mental by-paths, it has defeated its own end. To judge whether or not a particular illustration is likely to do that for any number of people in the congregation is not simple, and people vary, of course, in the ease with which their

[35] Cf., e.g., *Vanity Fair*, Chapter VI.

minds can be diverted. But the skillful illustrator recognizes the danger and uses no illustration, and no more of an illustration than his practical purpose requires.

One of the commonest ways in which attention can be diverted from a sermon theme is to employ as an illustration a story or an incident which, however true it may be, *sounds untrue.* To leave a congregation feeling, " That is a tall one! " is fatal to a preacher's purpose.

I was preaching one Christmas morning on the birth of our Lord. I wanted to make the familiar point (by way of beginning) that many people were so absorbed in the celebrations of Christmas that they forgot what it was they were celebrating. I began with an illustration:

" I remember being invited to a party held to celebrate a wedding. I arrived late and I knew nobody there but the friend who had invited me, and my part in the proceedings was little more than that of a spectator. Everybody seemed to be in high spirits. They danced and shouted and sang and laughed and played games, and indulged in heaps of harmless fun. They flung streamers across the hall, they chased after air balls, they pranced about in paper caps, they visited the sideboard for drinks, and young and old alike were reduced to a state of childish gaiety.

" Presently I noticed a young lady sitting in a corner alone. She seemed very happy, and smiled pleasantly when I caught her eye, but I thought she seemed a bit neglected, and I whispered to my friend, ' Who's the young lady in the corner? '

" ' Don't you know? ' he said, somewhat startled. ' I must introduce you. That's the bride.' "

That story was true and unexaggerated in a single detail. It provided a fitting opening for a sermon that was to stress (in part) the peril of elbowing Christ from the center of Christmas celebrations. It had one serious defect — as I discovered when worship was over. It *sounded* improbable. The people roguishly hinted that I had retouched the incident to suit my homiletical need. While I was striding on with my exposition, the minds of many of them had dawdled in the dance hall, and they were toying in their minds with the dubious absurdity of the forgotten bride.

One can use the most astonishing and improbable material for an illustration *if it is an undisputed fact*, e.g., some little-known truth of science, or some half-incredible incident of biography, clearly set down in the " definitive life." But when the illustration is drawn from personal experience, or belongs to the anecdotal class (little stories that float around but the truth of which it is impossible to confirm), let a man remember that it must not only *be* true but *sound* true. In no other way, with this kind of illustration, can he hope to keep the interest fixed upon the theme.

It will confirm the truth of this from a quite different angle if one glances back at the illustrative use of parables. Parables may be pure fiction but they *must* be free of all improbabilities. The experiences they express are almost commonplace. Every man knows the truth of them in his own soul. He may never have gone to the far country — not actually: he has gone in his heart. He may never have called his brother " this *thy son* " to his father's face: he has said it in his heart.

That is one of the most amazing things about the parable when used by the Master. It is all so ordinary — and so sublime. No man ever listened to the parable of the Prodigal Son and thought, " What a tall story! " It carries conviction. It doesn't even raise the question of its own truth. It is true to earth and heaven at the same time.

We may leave it there. If to some who read these pages it all seems much ado about nothing, a darkening, even, of counsel with words, I can only add my conviction that preaching the good news of Jesus Christ is the highest, holiest activity to which a man can give himself: a task which angels might envy and for which archangels might forsake the court of heaven. And because the craft of illustration has its own modest but not unimportant place in preaching, no man need regret a little time given to its close study.

The rules, no doubt, have their exceptions but the hour for the exception is best known to the people who best know the rules.

Yet, at the last, preaching is not just religious speaking; not the art of making a sermon and delivering it, but rather making a preacher and delivering Christ through him. Therefore, it will not be resented if I remind my readers in parting from them that our most impressive illustration in the end is ourselves:

" Lord, have mercy upon us.
Christ, have mercy upon us.
Lord, have mercy upon us."

INDEX

Index

Aesop, p. 30.

Allegory, p. 26; compared with fable and parable, pp. 29–30.

Analogy, pp. 26, 27–29.

Anecdote, 26; distinguished from biographical incident, p. 43; its dangers in preaching, pp. 43, 108–110.

Beecher, H. W., his method in illustration, p. 57.

Bible, as source of illustrations, pp. 53–54.

Biographical incident, pp. 26, 36–40. *See also* General Reading.

Bok, E., pp. 38–39.

Booth, William, p. 38.

Brooks, Phillips, defended ornamental use of illustrations, p. 23.

Bunyan, John, his use of allegory, p. 30.

Campion, Edmund, pp. 39–40.

Carlyle, Thomas, quotation, p. 15.

Chamberlain, Joseph, defense of R. W. Dale, p. 41.

Children, their quaint remarks supply illustrations, p. 75.

Church, Dean, illustrated rarely, p. 17.

Commonplace books. *See* Filing and Indexing.

Curie, Ève, comparison of indexes, pp. 81–84.

Dale, R. W., pp. 17, 24; use of personal experience in illustration, pp. 41–42. *See also* Chamberlain, J.

Denney, James, quotation, p. 111.

Dickens, Charles, p. 37.

Drummond, Henry, his use of figure of speech, p. 27.

Eliot, George, preoccupation with moral issues, p. 73.

Emerson, R. W., pp. 38–39.

Encyclopedias of illustrations, their danger, pp. 46–47.